NAVIGATING PASTORAL TRANSITIONS:
A PASTORAL SEARCH COMMITTEE HANDBOOK

John W. Utley
Doctor of Ministry

Cotton House Press

Navigating Pastoral Transitions:
A Pastoral Search Committee Handbook

By John W. Utley, D.Min.

Cotton House Press Books are published by

Cotton House Press, LLC
640 Taylor Street, Suite 1200
Fort Worth, Texas 76102
Visit our website at www.cottonhouse.press

ISBN: 979-8-9897607-4-9

Printed in United States of America
First Edition: June 1, 2024

Dr. John W. Utley, an ordained minister with the Assemblies of God, boasts over thirty-five years of pastoral experience. His extensive service extends beyond the pulpit to include participation on various boards and active engagement in mentoring roles. Dr. Utley is recognized as an authority on strategic organizational change, with a particular specialization in guiding transitions for businesses, churches, and non-profit entities. He is available for consultation and can be reached via email at john.utley@cottonhouse.press or by telephone at 574-370-3661.

Dedication

My love to Susan,
My Friend,
The Love of My Life,
My Greatest Cheerleader
My Most Compassionate Critic
The Perfect Wife.

There are dozens of family and friends who support, encourage, celebrate, and enable me to pursue my God-given purpose. To that end, I dedicate this book to those who have been my greatest cheerleaders: my beautiful wife, Susan; our children and their families: Joanna, Bobby and Maleah Federe; Jonathan and Jordan Utley; Joshua, Chelsea, Jesse and Elias; and my best friends, Tim & Debbie Boyd. I love you all and thank God daily for you!

Contents

Navigating Pastoral Transitions

Purpose of the Handbook

Introduction

1 Corinthians 15:58

"So, my dear brothers and sisters, be strong and immovable. Always work enthusiastically for the Lord, for you know that nothing you do for the Lord is ever useless (NLT)."

Transitioning to a new lead pastor is one of the most critical moments in the life of a church. Finding the right candidate who meets the needs of both the congregation and the community is not just a task—it's a mission of eternal significance. While this event may be rare for many churches, its importance cannot be overstated. The process can seem overwhelming, and church boards often feel unprepared for the challenge.

However, this handbook is here to empower and equip your Pastoral Search Committee with confidence and clarity. Despite the multitude of ministers seeking positions, locating the right pastor can feel as elusive as legendary creatures like the Loch Ness monster or Bigfoot. For denominationally affiliated churches, there may be more structure and support, but the task is still significant. For unaffiliated congregations, the responsibility is even greater.

In every scenario, the key to success lies in prayer, focus, and intentionality. This manual provides a step-by-step guide to navigating the pastoral search process, complete with templates, workflows, samples, and resources to ensure a smooth and efficient transition. While the procedures outlined here are methodical and precise, they must be underpinned by spiritual discernment and divine guidance. Remember the promise in Proverbs 3:5-6, "Trust in the LORD with all your heart; do not depend on your own understanding. Seek his will in all you do, and he will show you which path to take."

Think of this manual as the engine of your process, the search committee as the transmission that drives the vehicle, and prayer as the fuel that empowers the entire journey. With this handbook, you are equipped to move your church forward with confidence and faith, knowing that you are guided by a well-structured process and the wisdom of the Holy Spirit.

Involving a Transition Specialist

To navigate the pastoral transition process effectively, consider engaging a neutral third party to guide the Pastoral Search Committee. This specialist brings objectivity and expertise that can prevent the committee from making reactionary decisions based on the strengths or weaknesses of the previous lead pastor. Without this neutrality, there's a risk of bias, especially if the former pastor left due to moral or ethical failures, potentially leading to overlooked weaknesses in new candidates.

A transition specialist can objectively review the committee's processes and ensure a healthy, balanced approach throughout the search. This individual should possess both the necessary educational background and real-world experience in managing transitions, offering invaluable counsel to the committee.

To formalize this relationship, draft a Memorandum of Understanding (MOU) that clearly outlines the scope of the specialist's assistance and the parameters of their counsel. It's crucial that the transition specialist is not considered for the permanent pastoral position, as this could compromise their trustworthiness and objectivity.

If the specialist also serves as an interim pastor, explicitly define this dual role in the MOU, detailing office hours and interactions with the staff. This clarity ensures that both the transition specialist, the church board, and the search committee fully understand the expectations.

Finally, clearly communicate these roles and responsibilities to the congregation and staff to maintain unity and transparency throughout the transition process.

Prayer and Fasting

Before beginning this transition journey, encourage the congregation to participate in a time of prayer and fasting. The addendum includes a sample 21-day prayer guide, but you may use any format that best suits your congregation. The value of this phase cannot be overstated. As noted earlier, prayer is the fuel and provides the spiritual undergirding from the congregation, which will advance the cause of the will of God in the Church.

In Psalm 25, David wrote, "O LORD, I give my life to you. I trust in you, my God! Do not let me be disgraced, or let my enemies rejoice in my defeat. No one who trusts in you will ever be disgraced, but disgrace comes to those who try to deceive others. Show me the right path, O LORD; point out the road for me to follow. Lead me by your truth and teach me, for you are the God who saves me. All day long I put my hope in you. Remember, O LORD, your compassion and unfailing love, which you have shown from long ages past."

Jesus said, "I tell you, you can pray for anything, and if you believe that you've received it, it will be yours (Mark 11:24, NLT)." How much more will God do for His Church when we ask Him for help for this journey?

Consultation

Should you require further consultation, please feel free to reach out to the author. The first consultation is complimentary. Additionally, if you are using this guide, please inform the author so that he can pray for your journey toward discerning God's will for your congregation.

By following these guidelines and remaining diligent in prayer and communication, you will help ensure a smooth and faithful transition for your church.

Communication During the Pastoral Transition

The pastoral transition is a pivotal stage in the church's life. The congregation entrusts the pastoral search committee with the responsibility of recruiting and selecting a candidate who aligns with the church's established criteria. To foster an atmosphere of unity and trust throughout this process, the committee must provide regular updates on their progress and timelines. Transparent communication will help ensure that the congregation remains informed, engaged, and supportive during this significant period.

Overview of the Transition Process

The transition process for selecting a new lead pastor includes several vital phases: forming the committee, preparing for the search, evaluating candidates, selecting the final candidate, and ensuring a smooth onboarding process. Each phase is designed to provide a thorough and prayerful approach to finding the right leader for the congregation. Here is a description of each phase.

Forming the Pastoral Search Committee

The first phase involves forming a Pastoral Search Committee. This step is crucial as it sets the path forward for the church. This section details the selection criteria for committee members, their roles and responsibilities, and the initial meeting agenda.

Preparation Phase

In the preparation phase, the committee should review the congregation's mission and vision to maintain alignment with the church's direction. This phase includes surveying the congregation, creating a church profile, and defining the ideal candidate. These tasks provide valuable information for the committee and serve as resources for potential candidates.

Search Process

During the search process, the committee will develop or refine the job description for the lead pastor, advertise the position, and establish confidentiality and ethical guidelines. This phase also involves receiving and acknowledging applications, ensuring a fair and transparent process.

Candidate Evaluation

The candidate evaluation phase begins with screening applications, conducting preliminary interviews, running background checks, and contacting references. During this stage, the committee will shortlist potential candidates.

Interview Process

The interview process involves developing interview questions, conducting in-depth interviews, assessing preaching skills and pastoral care, and possibly visiting the candidate's current church. This comprehensive evaluation helps the committee make an informed decision.

Final Selection

In the final selection phase, the committee deliberates and chooses a candidate for the lead pastor role. Once a decision is made, the candidate is presented to the church leadership and staff, followed by a get-acquainted weekend and congregational approval.

Transition and Onboarding

After selecting a pastor, ensuring a smooth transition and onboarding is crucial. The committee should prepare the congregation, welcome the new pastor and their family, and provide an onboarding guide to ease the transition. Identifying point people to support the new pastor during the first six months is essential for a successful start.

Evaluation of the Transition Process

Finally, the committee should evaluate the transition process, gather feedback from the congregation, and document insights for future transitions. This reflection helps improve the process and ensures a strong foundation for future pastoral changes.

This manual provides a clear and detailed guide through each of these phases, helping to ensure a thoughtful, prayerful, and effective transition for the church.

Phase One: Forming the Pastoral Search Committee

Steps in Forming a Pastoral Search Committee

Introduction

Forming a pastoral search committee is critical in selecting a new lead pastor. This document outlines the steps in creating the committee, the selection criteria for its members, their roles and responsibilities, and the initial meeting agenda. The following steps are suggested. The constitution and bylaws always supersede these steps. In most cases, the official church board will be the nominating committee.

Step 1: Identify the Need for a Search Committee

- **Action:** Recognize the need for a new lead pastor and the importance of forming a search committee.

- **Responsible Parties:** Church board, existing church leadership.

Step 2: Determine the Size and Composition of the Committee

- **Action:** Decide the number of members to serve on the search committee.

- **Key Considerations:** Aim for a diverse group that represents the various demographics and ministries of the church.

- **Responsible Parties:** Church board.

Step 3: Establish Selection Criteria for Committee Members

- **Action:** Define the qualities and qualifications desired in search committee members (see sample below).

- **Key Considerations:** Commitment to the church's mission, understanding of its vision, ability to work collaboratively, and confidentiality.

- **Responsible Parties:** Church board, nominating committee.

Selection Criteria for Committee Members (Sample)

- **Commitment to the Church's Mission and Vision:** Members should actively support the church's mission and vision.

- **Diverse Representation:** Include members from various demographics (age, gender, ethnicity, etc.) and ministry areas (youth, worship, outreach, etc.).

- **Spiritual Maturity:** Members should exhibit a strong, mature faith grounded in prayer and biblical principles.

- **Collaborative Spirit:** Ability to work well with others, respect differing viewpoints, and seek consensus.

- **Confidentiality:** Maintain strict confidentiality regarding the search process and candidate information.

- **Leadership and Communication Skills:** Effective in leading discussions and communicating clearly with the committee and congregation.

Step 4: Nominate and Select Committee Members

- **Action:** Nominate and select individuals who meet the established criteria. Appoint individuals for the five roles defined on page 13; the remaining members are voting members with no defined role.

- **Key Considerations:** Seek input from church leadership and congregation.

- **Responsible Parties:** Church board, nominating committee.

Step 5: Commission the Search Committee

- **Action:** Officially appoint and commission the search committee.

- **Key Considerations:** Publicly recognize the committee and its mandate.

- **Responsible Parties:** Church board.

Roles and Responsibilities of Committee Members

Chairperson (this may be the transition specialist if the church has retained one):

- **Responsibilities:** Lead meetings, coordinate the search process, communicate with candidates, and serve as the primary liaison with the church board. If the chairperson is the transition specialist, they would be a non-voting search committee member.

- **Skills Needed:** Leadership, organization, communication.

Vice-Chairperson:

- **Responsibilities:** Assist the chairperson, lead meetings in their absence, and support coordination efforts.

- **Skills Needed:** Leadership, organization.

Secretary:

- **Responsibilities:** Take detailed meeting minutes, manage documentation, and ensure proper record-keeping.

- **Skills Needed:** Attention to detail, organizational skills.

Communications Coordinator:

- **Responsibilities:** Manage communication with the congregation, provide updates, and handle publicity related to the search process.

- **Skills Needed:** Communication, marketing, public relations.

Prayer Coordinator:

- **Responsibilities:** Lead prayer initiatives for the search process, organize prayer meetings, and ensure the committee remains spiritually grounded.

- **Skills Needed:** Spiritual maturity, leadership in prayer.

Committee Members:

- **Responsibilities:** Participate in meetings, review candidate applications, conduct interviews, and provide input throughout the search process.

- **Skills Needed:** Discernment, collaboration, commitment.

Initial Meeting Agenda for Search Committee Members

Once committee members are selected, the initial meeting sets the tone for all future committee meetings. The chairperson should guide the meeting, ensuring that the agenda is followed thoroughly, and the committee members are treated with respect. Honor their time by ensuring the meeting goes within the stated time frame. The following agenda is designed as a two-hour overview initial meeting.

Opening and Welcome

- **Time:** 10 minutes
- **Lead:** Chairperson
- **Purpose:** Introduce members, outline the meeting agenda, and establish a positive and collaborative tone.

Devotional and Prayer

- **Time:** 15 minutes
- **Lead:** Prayer Coordinator
- **Purpose:** Begin with a devotional message and prayer to seek God's guidance in the search process.

Introduction to the Search Process

- **Time:** 20 minutes
- **Lead:** Chairperson
- **Purpose:** Provide an overview of the pastoral search process, including key stages and timelines.

Roles and Responsibilities

- **Time:** 20 minutes
- **Lead:** Chairperson

- **Purpose:** Outline the roles and responsibilities of each committee member, emphasizing the importance of confidentiality and collaboration.

Review of Selection Criteria

- **Time:** 15 minutes
- **Lead:** Chairperson
- **Purpose:** Discuss the criteria for evaluating candidates and ensure alignment with the church's needs and vision.

Communication Plan

- **Time:** 20 minutes
- **Lead:** Communications Coordinator
- **Purpose:** Develop a plan for communicating with the congregation, including regular updates and ways to involve the church in prayer.

Initial Tasks and Assignments

- **Time:** 20 minutes
- **Lead:** Chairperson
- **Purpose:** Assign initial tasks, such as drafting the job description, creating the church profile, and setting up a candidate review process.

Q&A and Open Discussion

- **Time:** 15 minutes
- **Lead:** Chairperson
- **Purpose:** Allow committee members to ask questions and discuss any concerns or ideas they have.

Closing Prayer

- **Time:** 5 minutes
- **Lead:** Prayer Coordinator

- **Purpose:** Close the meeting with prayer, asking for wisdom and unity as the committee begins its work.

Adjournment

- **Time:**
- **Lead:** Chairperson
- **Purpose:** Officially end the meeting and outline the next steps.

Conclusion:

Forming a pastoral search committee with clear selection criteria, defined roles and responsibilities, and a structured initial meeting agenda sets the foundation for a successful search process. Following these steps, the committee can work together to find the best candidate for the lead pastor position.

Phase Two: The Preparation Phase

Introduction

In this stage, the committee will review the Church's Mission and Vision and conduct congregational and search committee assessments to determine the qualities desired in a lead pastor. The mission and vision inform the search as much as the felt needs of the committee and the church. This is the first step of a comprehensive overview of the church that will be completed later.

The following information is critical for this process.

Church Information Worksheet for Potential Lead Pastoral Candidate

Church Overview

- Church Name: [Church Name]
- Address: [Church Address]
- Website: [Church Website]
- Contact Information:
- Phone: [Church Phone Number]
- Email: [Church Email Address]

Church Description

- Mission Statement: [Insert the church's mission statement here.]
- Vision Statement: [Insert the church's vision statement here.]
- Core Values:
- [Core Value 1]
- [Core Value 2]
- [Core Value 3]
- [Core Value 4]
- [Core Value 5]

Conducting a Congregational Survey

Conducting a comprehensive church survey will guide the search committee in selecting candidates who align with the congregation's needs. This achieves two important objectives. First, it informs the committee about the desires and expectations of church members regarding a lead pastor. Second, it makes the congregation feel integral to the selection process, ensuring their views are considered and validated.

Comprehensive Church Survey and Assessment Questionnaire

Introduction

This survey and assessment questionnaire is designed to gather valuable input from church members and the pastoral search committee. The responses will help identify the needs and requirements for the new Lead Pastor of [Church Name]. Your honest and thoughtful answers are greatly appreciated and will play a crucial role in shaping the future leadership of our church. The feedback in this questionnaire will be provided to the search committee for use as they search for our next lead pastor.

Part 1: Church Member Survey

General Information

Name (Optional):_____

Age Group:
- Under 18
- 18-25
- 26-35
- 36-45
- 46-55
- 56-65
- 66 and above

How long have you been attending [Church Name]?

- Less than 1 year
- 1-3 years
- 4-7 years
- 8-10 years
- More than 10 years

Church Involvement

Which ministries or activities are you involved in at [Church Name]? (Check all that apply)

- o Worship Team
- o Children's Ministry
- o Youth Ministry
- o Small Groups
- o Outreach and Missions
- o Hospitality
- o Other (Please specify):

_____

_____

_____

Worship and Preaching

How would you describe the current worship style at [Church Name]?

- o Traditional
- o Contemporary
- o Blended

Other   (Please   specify):

_____

What elements of the worship service are most meaningful to you? (Check all that apply)

- o Music
- o Prayer
- o Sermon
- o Communion
- o Fellowship
- o Other (Please specify): _____

How would you rate the current preaching/teaching at [Church Name]?

- o Excellent
- o Good
- o Fair
- o Poor

Church Leadership and Community

What qualities do you believe are most important in a Lead Pastor? (Check up to 5)

- o Strong Preaching and Teaching
- o Visionary Leadership
- o Pastoral Care and Counseling
- o Administrative Skills

- o Community Engagement
- o Spiritual Maturity
- o Ability to Connect with All Age Groups

Other (Please specify):

_____

_____

_____

How important is it for the new Lead Pastor to be involved in community outreach and engagement?

- o Very Important
- o Important
- o Somewhat Important
- o Not Important

Analysis of the Church

What do you see as the greatest strengths of [Church Name]?

_____

_____

_____

What areas do you believe [Church Name] needs to improve or develop?

_____

_____

_____

Future Vision and Goals

What is your vision for the future of [Church Name]?

_____

_____

_____

What specific goals do you think the new Lead Pastor should focus on in their first year?

_____

_____

_____

Is there anything else you would like to share about the needs and requirements for the new Lead Pastor?

_____

_____

_____

Pastoral Search Committee Assessment

Introduction

The search committee should also complete an assessment to establish the criteria for a lead pastor at the church. This should be done individually, and the results tabulated for review later.

Leadership and Administration

What leadership style do you believe will be most effective for the new Lead Pastor at [Church Name]?

- o Collaborative
- o Authoritative
- o Servant Leadership
- o Other (Please specify):

_____

What administrative skills are essential for the new Lead Pastor?

_____

_____

_____

What preaching and teaching methods are most needed to address the current needs of our congregation?

_____

_____

_____

How can the new Lead Pastor enhance the spiritual growth and discipleship within the church?

_____

_____

_____

What are the key areas of pastoral care and counseling that need to be prioritized?

_____

_____

_____

How should the new Lead Pastor approach conflict resolution and mediation within the church?

_____

_____

_____

Community Engagement and Outreach

What specific community outreach initiatives should the new Lead Pastor champion?

_____

_____

_____

How can the new Lead Pastor strengthen the church's presence and impact in the local community?

_____

_____

_____

Vision and Strategic Planning

What strategic goals should the new Lead Pastor set for the next 3-5 years?

_____

_____

_____

What resources and support will the new Lead Pastor need to achieve these goals?

_____

_____

_____

Personal and Spiritual Characteristics

What personal and spiritual characteristics are essential for the new Lead Pastor?

_____

_____

_____

How important is it for the new Lead Pastor to have a strong presence in church activities and events?

- o Very Important
- o Important
- o Somewhat Important
- o Not Important

Final Thoughts

What additional insights or suggestions do you have for selecting the new Lead Pastor?

_____

_____

_____

Thank you for your participation in this important survey. Your feedback will be instrumental in helping us find the right leader for [Church Name].

Contact Information for Follow-Up (Optional):

Name: _____

Phone: _____

Email: _____

Please return this survey to [Designated Person or Drop-Off Location] by [Due Date].

Expectations Guide for Lead Pastor Position

Instructions

This guide is designed to gather input from church members and pastoral search committee members regarding the desired professional qualities and expectations for the next Lead Pastor of [Church Name]. Please rank the listed qualities and expectations in order of importance, with 1 being the most important and 8 being the least important. Additionally, use the "Other" section to list any specific expectations not covered in the provided categories.

Desired Professional Qualities

Instructions

Rank the following professional qualities in order of importance (1 = most important, 8 = least important).

_____Strong Preaching and Teaching

Ability to deliver engaging and biblically sound sermons that inspire, encourage, and educate the congregation.

_____Visionary Leadership

Capacity to develop and communicate a clear vision for the church's future, fostering growth and development.

_____Pastoral Care and Counseling

Proficiency in providing spiritual support, counseling, and care to individuals and families within the congregation.

_____Administrative Skills

Competence in managing church operations, finances, and staff effectively.

_____Community Engagement

Commitment to engaging with and serving the local community, representing the church positively.

_____Spiritual Maturity

Demonstrates a deep and growing personal relationship with Christ, embodying the church's core values.

_____Ability to Connect with All Age Groups

Skill in relating to and engaging with congregants of all ages, from children to seniors.

_____Conflict Resolution

Ability to mediate and resolve conflicts within the church in a constructive and compassionate manner.

Other Specific Expectations

Please list any additional qualities, skills, or expectations you have for the next Lead Pastor that are not covered in the above categories:

_____

_____

_____

Please provide any additional comments or insights you have regarding the selection of the next Lead Pastor:

_____

_____

_____

Thank you for your participation. Your feedback is crucial in helping us find the right leader for [Church Name].

Please return this guide to [Designated Person or Drop-Off Location] by [Due Date].

Church Information Worksheet for Potential Lead Pastoral Candidate

Creating a Church Profile Document the church's history, mission, vision, programs, and community involvement is crucial to the pastoral search committee for reference and the pastoral candidate for context.

Complete the following using the previous worksheet:

Church Overview

- Church Name: [Church Name]
- Address: [Church Address]
- Website: [Church Website]
- Contact Information:
- Phone: [Church Phone Number]
- Email: [Church Email Address]

Church Description

- Mission Statement: [Insert the church's mission statement here.]
- Vision Statement: [Insert the church's vision statement here.]

Core Values:

- [Core Value 1]
- [Core Value 2]
- [Core Value 3]
- [Core Value 4]
- [Core Value 5]

Now, compile the following information for a comprehensive overview of the church and community.

Church History

Founding Year: [Year the church was founded]

Key Milestones:

1. [Year and Event]
2. [Year and Event]
3. [Year and Event]
4. Notable Achievements:
5. [Achievement 1]
6. [Achievement 2]
7. [Achievement 3]

Summary: [Provide a brief narrative summary of the church's history, highlighting significant events and changes over the years.]

Church Strengths

1. Strong Congregational Engagement: [Describe the level of involvement and engagement from the congregation.]

2. Diverse Ministry Programs: [List and briefly describe key ministry programs, such as children's ministry, youth ministry, adult education, etc.]

3. Vibrant Worship Services: [Describe the style and atmosphere of the church's worship services.]

4. Community Outreach: [Detail the church's involvement in community service and outreach programs.]

5. Supportive Leadership Team: [Provide information on the current church leadership structure and team.]

Church Challenges

1. Membership Retention: [Discuss any challenges related to retaining members and maintaining attendance.]

2. Financial Sustainability: [Outline any financial challenges the church is facing.]

3. Facility Maintenance: [Describe any issues or needed improvements related to the church building and facilities.]

4. Community Engagement: [Identify challenges in connecting with and serving the local community.]

5. Program Development: [Mention any difficulties in expanding or developing new ministry programs.]

Community Description

- Community Name: [Name of the community or neighborhood where the church is located]

- Location: [Brief description of the church's geographical location]

Demographics:

- Population: [Number of people living in the community]

- Age Distribution: [Breakdown of age groups in the community]

- Cultural Diversity: [Description of the cultural and ethnic diversity within the community]

Local Economy:

- Major Employers: [List major employers and industries in the area]

- Economic Overview: [Brief description of the local economy, including employment rates and key economic activities]

Community Strengths:

- Education: [Describe the quality and availability of educational institutions in the area]

- Healthcare: [Provide information on local healthcare facilities and services]

- Recreation: [Detail recreational opportunities, parks, and community centers]

Community Challenges:

- Economic Disparities: [Discuss any economic challenges or disparities within the community]

- Social Issues: [Identify social issues such as crime rates, homelessness, or substance abuse]

- Infrastructure: [Describe any challenges related to local infrastructure, such as transportation or housing]

Conclusion

Summary:

[Provide a brief summary of the church's current state, its goals for the future, and how the potential Lead Pastor can contribute to achieving these goals.]

Next Steps: [Outline the next steps in the pastoral selection process and any additional information the candidate should expect to receive.]

Contact Information for Follow-Up:
- Search Committee Chair:
- Name: [Chair's Name]

- Phone: [Chair's Phone Number]
- Email: [Chair's Email Address]

- Church Office:
- Phone: [Church Office Phone Number]
- Email: [Church Office Email Address]

Attachments:

- Church Constitution and Bylaws
- Most Recent Annual Report
- Chamber of Commerce Community Profile

Please return this worksheet with any additional questions or comments you may have about our church and community.

Ideal Candidate Profile for Lead Pastor

Introduction

Defining the Ideal Candidate Profile based on the survey results and church profile, create a profile of the ideal candidate, including qualities, experience, and theological alignment is a crucial step in evaluating candidates.

This document outlines the ideal candidate for the Lead Pastor position at [Church Name]. This profile will guide the Pastoral Search Committee in identifying and evaluating candidates who align with the church's mission, vision, and values.

Candidate Profile

Spiritual and Personal Qualities

1. **Deep Faith and Spiritual Maturity**
   - **Attributes:** Demonstrates a deep and abiding relationship with Jesus Christ, evidenced by a life of prayer, personal Bible study, and spiritual disciplines.
   - **Indicators:** Personal testimony, spiritual practices, references from spiritual mentors.

2. **Integrity and Character**
   - **Attributes:** Exhibits high moral standards, honesty, and ethical behavior.
   - **Indicators:** Background checks, references, personal interviews.

3. **Passion for Ministry**
   - **Attributes:** Displays a genuine passion for preaching, teaching, and pastoral care.
   - **Indicators:** Previous ministry experience, sermon evaluations, candidate's vision for ministry.

Theological and Doctrinal Alignment

1. **Sound Theological Understanding**
   - **Attributes:** Holds a strong grasp of biblical theology and adheres to the church's doctrinal statements.
   - **Indicators:** Theological education, doctrinal questionnaire, doctrinal statement.

2. **Commitment to the Church's Denomination**
   - **Attributes:** Aligns with the theological and ecclesiastical stance of the church's denomination.
   - **Indicators:** Denominational involvement, theological interviews.

Leadership and Vision

1. **Visionary Leadership**
   - **Attributes:** Possesses the ability to cast a compelling vision for the church's future and inspire others to follow.
   - **Indicators:** Vision casting examples, leadership experience, strategic planning skills.

2. **Strategic Thinker**
   - **Attributes:** Capable of developing and implementing strategic plans to achieve the church's mission and goals.

- **Indicators:** Previous strategic initiatives, problem-solving skills, adaptability.

3. Effective Communicator

- **Attributes:** Skilled in preaching, teaching, and communicating effectively with diverse audiences.
- **Indicators:** Sermon evaluations, communication style, public speaking experience.

Pastoral Care and Relational Skills

1. Shepherd's Heart

- **Attributes:** Shows genuine love and care for the congregation, prioritizing pastoral care and counseling.
- **Indicators:** Pastoral care experience, references from congregants, personal testimonies.

2. Strong Interpersonal Skills

- **Attributes:** Builds and maintains healthy relationships with staff, congregants, and community members.
- **Indicators:** Conflict resolution examples, team-building experience, relational aptitude.

3. Diversity

- **Attributes:** Values, promotes, and embraces the diversity within the congregation and community.
- **Indicators:** Experience in diverse settings, commitment to diversity.

Administrative and Organizational Abilities

1. **Effective Administrator**
   - **Attributes:** Demonstrates strong administrative skills, including budgeting, planning, and organizational management.
   - **Indicators:** Previous administrative experience, references, organizational achievements.

2. **Team Leadership**
   - **Attributes:** Capable of leading and mentoring church staff and volunteer leaders.
   - **Indicators:** Leadership evaluations, team development examples, staff testimonials.

Outreach and Community Engagement

1. **Evangelistic Passion**
   - **Attributes:** Committed to outreach, evangelism, and community engagement.
   - **Indicators:** Outreach initiatives, evangelism training, community involvement.

Community Connector

   - **Attributes:** Builds bridges between the church and the local community, fostering partnerships and outreach opportunities.
   - **Indicators:** Community projects, partnerships with local organizations, community impact.

Family and Personal Life

1. **Supportive Family**
   - **Attributes:** Maintains a healthy and supportive family life that aligns with the pastoral calling.

- **Indicators:** Family involvement in ministry, spousal support, family health.

2. **Work-Life Balance**
   - **Attributes:** Prioritizes personal well-being and maintains a healthy work-life balance.
   - **Indicators:** Personal self-care practices, previous work-life balance, references.

Conclusion

The ideal candidate for the Lead Pastor position should demonstrate a strong spiritual foundation, effective leadership skills, and a commitment to the church's mission and vision. By adhering to this profile, the Pastoral Search Committee can ensure a thorough and effective search process, ultimately selecting a pastor who will lead the church with wisdom, integrity, and a heart for ministry.

Phase Three: The Search Process

Introduction

In this phase, you will develop or fine-tune a job description for a lead pastor for your congregation. If you already have a job description, fine tune it for your search committee's use. If you do not have a job description, the addendum contains three job descriptions for large, medium, and smaller churches. Feel free to tailor these to suit the context of your congregation.

Once you have established a comprehensive picture of your ideal candidate, you can begin the search process. The first step for the process is to advertise for the position of lead pastor. To prepare the search committee for this phase, it is vital that everyone understands and agrees to the following confidentiality and ethical guidelines. Please review them and ask the committee members to sign that they understand and agree to the guidelines.

Confidentiality and Ethical Guidelines for Pastoral Search Committees

Selecting a new lead pastor is a sacred responsibility that requires the utmost care, discretion, and adherence to ethical principles. As members of the pastoral search committee, it is crucial to maintain confidentiality and uphold the highest standards of integrity throughout the process. This document outlines the confidentiality and ethical guidelines, as well as best practices, to ensure a fair, transparent, and God-honoring search.

Confidentiality Guidelines

1. **Candidate Information:** All information related to potential candidates, including resumes, references, and personal details, must be treated with strict confidentiality. This information should only be shared with authorized members of the search committee and church leadership on a need-to-know basis.

2. **Committee Deliberations:** Discussions and deliberations within the search committee should remain confidential. Committee members should refrain from sharing details about the candidates or the decision-making process with individuals outside the committee.

3. **Secure Storage and Disposal:** Any physical or digital documents containing candidate information should be stored securely and disposed of properly once the search process is complete.

4. **Non-Disclosure Agreements:** Consider having search committee members sign non-disclosure agreements to reinforce the importance of confidentiality and protect the privacy of candidates.

Ethical Guidelines

1. **Fairness and Impartiality:** Treat all candidates with fairness, respect, and impartiality, regardless of their background, race, gender, or other personal characteristics. Ensure that the evaluation process is free from bias or discrimination.

2. **Transparency and Honesty:** Be transparent and honest in all communications with candidates. Provide accurate information about the church, the position, and the search process. Avoid making promises or commitments that cannot be fulfilled.

3. **Respect for Candidates' Privacy:** Respect the privacy of candidates and refrain from discussing their personal information or circumstances outside of the search committee.

4. **Conflict of Interest:** Disclose any potential conflicts of interest that may arise during the search process. Committee members should recuse themselves from discussions or decisions where a conflict of interest exists.

5. **Integrity in References and Background Checks:** Conduct thorough reference checks and background checks with integrity and respect for the candidates' privacy. Obtain proper consent and follow all applicable laws and regulations.

6. **Prayerful Discernment:** Seek God's guidance and wisdom throughout the search process through prayer and spiritual discernment. Rely on the leading of the Holy Spirit in making decisions.

Best Practices

1. **Establish Clear Criteria:** Develop a clear set of criteria for the lead pastor position, based on the church's vision, mission, and needs. Ensure that these criteria are consistently applied to all candidates.

2. **Maintain Detailed Records:** Keep detailed records of the search process, including candidate evaluations, committee deliberations, and decision-making rationale. This will ensure transparency and accountability.

3. **Provide Timely Communication:** Communicate with candidates in a timely and professional manner, keeping them informed about the status of their application and the search process.

4. **Seek Counsel and Support:** If needed, seek counsel from trusted advisors, such as denominational leaders or experienced search consultants, to ensure adherence to best practices and ethical standards.

5. **Celebrate and Support the New Lead Pastor:** Once the selection is made, celebrate the new lead pastor and provide them with the necessary support and resources to transition smoothly into their new role.

By adhering to these confidentiality and ethical guidelines, as well as implementing best practices, the pastoral search committee can navigate the selection process with integrity, professionalism, and a deep commitment to honoring God's will for the church.

Best Practices for Advertising a Lead Pastor Position at a Large Church

Introduction

Once the search committee has a comprehensive profile for a lead pastor candidate, and a firm understanding of the needs and desires of the church, the search may proceed. How does a church attract the best candidates for the position? Advertising through a variety of means will provide many possible prospects. The following best practices will encourage a process whereby the church may obtain the maximum number of applicants. The downside of too much advertising is that the church may solicit too many applicants and overwhelm the search committee.

If the church hires a search firm to solicit possible candidates, then the field of candidates is sourced from their database. If not, consider the following best practices for advertising the position.

I. **Develop a Comprehensive Job Description:**

A. Clearly outline the responsibilities, expectations, and goals for the lead pastor position.

B. Include detailed qualifications, required experience, and desired skills.

C. Highlight the church's mission, vision, and values to attract candidates who align with them.

II.   Utilize Multiple Advertising Channels:

A. Denominational Websites: Advertise on the job board or career section of your church's denominational website, as this will reach candidates who share your theological beliefs and values.

     1.   Example: [DenominationName].org/jobs

B. Christian Job Boards: Post the opening on popular Christian job boards, which are frequented by individuals seeking ministry positions.

     1.   Examples: ChurchStaffing.com,   ChristianCareerCenter.com, ChurchJobs.net

C.   Ministry and Leadership Websites

     1.   Local Church Websites: Reach out to churches within your denomination or network and request to have the job posting listed on their websites or shared with their congregations.

     2.   Ministry Leadership Websites: Advertise on websites focused on ministry leadership, as these platforms are visited by individuals interested in pastoral roles.

         a.   Examples: MinistryJobs.com,   MinistryResources.com, MinistryPay.com

D. Christian Leadership Blogs and Podcasts: Explore advertising opportunities on popular Christian leadership blogs or podcasts that align with your church's vision and values.

E. Social Media Platforms:

1. Facebook and Instagram: Utilize targeted advertising on social media platforms like Facebook and Instagram to reach potential candidates within specific geographic areas or demographics.

2. LinkedIn: Post the job opening on LinkedIn, which can be an effective platform for reaching professionals in ministry and leadership roles.

3. X (formerly known as Twitter): Share the job posting on your church's X (Twitter) account and engage with relevant hashtags (e.g., #MinistryJobs, #PastorSearch) to increase visibility.

F. **Local and Regional Advertising**

1. Local Christian Publications: Advertise in local Christian newspapers, magazines, or newsletters that are distributed within your community or region.

2. Local Christian Radio Stations: Consider advertising on local Christian radio stations, as these can reach a targeted audience within your geographic area.

G. **Leverage Professional Networks:**

1. Seminary and Bible College Career Centers: Contact seminaries and Bible colleges in your area or those aligned with your denomination, and inquire about advertising the position through their career centers or job boards.

IX. Create an Engaging Professional Promotional Video

A. Develop a video that showcases the church, its community, and the opportunities the position offers. Include testimonials from current staff and congregation members about the church culture and community impact.

X. Highlight Unique Selling Points:

A. Emphasize what makes your church unique, such as community programs, church growth, and involvement opportunities.

B. Highlight the church's support system, resources, and commitment to the pastor's well-being and professional development.

XI. Ensure Clear Application Instructions:

A. Provide detailed instructions on how to apply, including required documents (resume, cover letter, references, etc.).

B. Include a deadline for applications and an estimated timeline for the hiring process.

Conclusion:

To attract the best candidates for a lead pastor position at a large church, it is crucial to implement a range of effective advertising strategies. By following these best practices, the church can maximize its reach and attract a diverse pool of qualified applicants.

Communications Workflow for Prospective Lead Pastor Applicants

Introduction

Once the church begins receiving applications, it is vital to establish a workflow providing clear and consistent communication between the pastoral search committee and prospective lead pastor applicants. It includes templates for acknowledging receipt of applications, informing applicants of their status, and requesting additional information.

Workflow Steps

1. **Receipt of Application**
   - Action: Acknowledge receipt of the application or resume.
   - Timing: Within 2 business days of receiving the application.
   - Template: Letter A - Acknowledgment of Application Receipt.

2. **Initial Screening**
   - Action: Conduct initial screening of applications to determine if they meet the selection criteria.
   - Timing: Within 2 weeks of receiving the application.
   - Outcomes:
     - Proceed to Next Step: Applicant meets initial criteria.
     - Does Not Proceed: Applicant does not meet criteria.

3. **Informing Applicants of Initial Screening Results**
   - Action: Inform applicants of the results of the initial screening.
   - Timing: Within 3 business days after the initial screening decision.
   - Templates:

o Letter B - Applicant Did Not Meet Selection Criteria.

o Letter C - Request for Additional Information.

4. Request for Additional Information

- Action: Request applicants who meet initial criteria to answer additional questions.

- Timing: As soon as the decision to proceed is made.

- Template: Letter C - Request for Additional Information.

Letter Templates

Letter A: Acknowledgment of Application Receipt

Subject: Acknowledgment of Application Receipt

Dear [Applicant's Name],

Greetings in the name of our Lord Jesus Christ.

We have received your application for the position of Lead Pastor at [Church Name]. We are grateful for your interest in joining our church community, as well as the time and effort you have put into your application.

Our search committee is carefully reviewing all applications and will notify you of the next steps in the process within the next two weeks. We appreciate your patience during this time.

Thank you once again for your interest in serving with us. May God bless you as you continue to seek His will for your ministry.

In Christ,

[Your Name]
[Title]
[Church Name]
[Contact Information]

Letter B: Applicant Did Not Meet Selection Criteria

Subject: Update on Your Application for Lead Pastor Position

Dear [Applicant's Name],

Greetings in the name of our Lord Jesus Christ.

Thank you for your application for the position of Lead Pastor at [Church Name]. After careful review and consideration, we regret to inform you that we will not be moving forward with your application at this time.

We greatly appreciate the time and effort you invested in your application and your desire to serve our church community. We pray that God will continue to guide and bless you in your ministry journey.

Thank you once again for your interest in [Church Name].

In Christ,

[Your Name]
[Title]
[Church Name]
[Contact Information]

Letter C: Request for Additional Information

Subject: Request for Additional Information for Lead Pastor Application

Dear [Applicant's Name],

Greetings in the name of our Lord Jesus Christ.

Thank you for your application for the position of Lead Pastor at [Church Name]. We have reviewed your initial application and are interested in learning more about your qualifications and vision for ministry.

To help us better understand your experience and approach to pastoral leadership, we kindly ask you to answer the following additional questions:

Question 1: [Insert Question]
Question 2: [Insert Question]
Question 3: [Insert Question]

Please send your responses to these questions by [specific date, typically within one week].

We appreciate your cooperation and look forward to learning more about you. Thank you once again for your interest in serving with us.

In Christ,
[Your Name]
[Title]
[Church Name]
[Contact Information]

Conclusion

By following this communications workflow and using the provided templates, the pastoral search committee can ensure clear, timely, and respectful communication with all applicants. This process helps maintain the integrity and efficiency of the search process while keeping applicants informed and engaged.

Phase Four: Candidate Evaluation

Initial Screening of Applications

Introduction

Evaluating applicants begins when the first resumes or applications arrive. The first initial step is to ensure the candidate meets the minimum qualifications.

Initial Screening Protocols for Lead Pastor Candidates

When searching for a new lead pastor, especially in a large church setting, it is essential to have a well-defined screening process to identify the most qualified and suitable candidates. This document outlines the initial screening protocols to be followed by the pastoral search committee.

Preliminary Review

1. **Minimum Qualifications Check:** Conduct an initial review of all applications to ensure that candidates meet the minimum qualifications outlined in the job description. This may include educational requirements, years of experience, and any specific certifications or licenses required.

2. **Theological Alignment:** Assess the candidate's theological beliefs and ensure they align with the church's doctrinal statement and denominational affiliation, if applicable.

3. **Mission and Vision Fit:** Evaluate the candidate's understanding of and alignment with the church's mission, vision, and core values.

At this stage, a candidate should not move forward in the process unless the minimum qualifications are met.

Application Materials Review

1. **Resume and Cover Letter:** Thoroughly review the candidate's resume and cover letter, paying attention to their educational background, ministry experience, leadership roles, and accomplishments.

2. **Sermon Samples:** Request and review sermon samples or recordings to assess the candidate's preaching style, biblical knowledge, and communication skills.

3. **Writing Samples:** Evaluate any writing samples provided, such as published articles, blog posts, or other written materials, to gauge the candidate's communication abilities and theological depth.

At this stage, the candidate should not move forward if they do not meet the criteria of the committee for the ideal candidate. Moving to the next phase requires contact with the potential candidates and their permission to move forward with background checks, reference checks, etc. The chairperson should communicate with all candidates that the search committee desires to move forward with their application and seek permission from the candidate to initialize the next steps in the process.

Background and Reference Checks

1. **Criminal Background Check:** Conduct a thorough criminal background check on candidates who advance to the next stage of the screening process. (Ministrysafe.com, protectmyministry.com, and other companies provide thorough background checks for potential candidates. Additionally, the church's insurance company may also provide this service).

2. **Reference Checks:** Follow up with the candidate's references, both professional and personal, to gather additional insights into their character, leadership abilities, and ministry effectiveness. See the addendum for suggested questions for reference checks.

3. **Social Media Review:** Review the candidate's public social media presence to ensure alignment with the church's values and to identify any potential concerns or red flags.

4. **Verification of Credentials:** Verify the candidate's educational credentials, ordination status, and any other relevant certifications or licenses.

By following these initial screening protocols, the pastoral search committee can effectively narrow down the candidate pool and identify the most promising individuals for further consideration. It is important to approach this process with diligence, discernment, and a commitment to finding the right leader who will guide the church in fulfilling its mission and vision.

Phase Five: Initial Interviews

Introduction

Once the initial screening has occurred, the committee should be able to "short-list" candidates. By this point, there should be at least three candidates who meet the initial criteria. The next phase is to begin to conduct the initial interviews. The following are considerations regarding interviews.

1. **Phone or Video Interviews:** Conduct initial phone or video interviews with candidates who meet the minimum qualifications and align with the church's theological beliefs and mission. These interviews follow the initial screening of applicants. These interviews should focus on assessing the candidate's communication skills, leadership abilities, and overall fit for the role.

2. **Interview Panel:** Establish an interview panel consisting of members of the search committee, church leadership, and potentially representatives from various ministries or congregational groups.

3. **Structured Interview Questions:** Develop a set of structured interview questions that address the candidate's qualifications, ministry philosophy, leadership style, and vision for the church.

4. **Evaluation Criteria:** Establish clear evaluation criteria for the initial interviews, considering factors such as theological alignment, leadership abilities, communication skills, and overall fit with the church's culture and needs.

Interview Process

Developing Interview Questions

Prepare a set of questions to evaluate candidates' fit with the church's needs and mission. Listed below are samples of questions. It would be wise for the search committee to tailor questions based on the context of the local congregation. Consider using two sets of questions, one for the initial interview, and the second, for the comprehensive interview.

Potential Pastoral Questions

Personal/Background Questions

1. Can you tell us about your journey to faith and what led you to pursue pastoral ministry?
2. What are your educational and professional qualifications, and how have they prepared you for this role?
3. Describe your previous pastoral experience. What did you learn from these experiences?
4. How do you balance your personal life and ministry responsibilities?
5. What books, authors, or leaders have most influenced your theology and ministry style?
6. What do you enjoy doing in your free time to recharge and relax?

Philosophy of Ministry Questions

1. How do you define the role of a lead pastor in the local church?
2. What is your approach to preaching and teaching? How do you prepare your sermons?
3. How do you incorporate discipleship into the life of the church?
4. What are your views on the role of worship in the church?
5. How do you balance the various responsibilities of pastoral ministry, such as preaching, teaching, counseling, and administration?
6. How do you handle theological disagreements within the congregation?
7. What is your approach to church growth and evangelism?
8. How do you view the role of lay leaders in the church?
9. What is your philosophy on church governance and decision-making processes?
10. How do you ensure your ministry remains relevant to contemporary issues and the needs of the congregation?
11. What role do spiritual gifts play in your ministry, and how do you help others discover and use their gifts?
12. How do you foster a sense of community and belonging within the church?

Spiritual Life of the Pastor Questions

1. How do you maintain your personal spiritual disciplines (prayer, Bible study, etc.)?
2. How do you ensure you are spiritually growing and not just maintaining?
3. Describe a time when you felt spiritually challenged and how you responded.
4. How do you seek spiritual accountability in your life and ministry?
5. What practices help you to hear and discern God's voice?
6. How do you guard against burnout and maintain your passion for ministry?
7. How do you integrate your spiritual life into your family life?

Outreach and Evangelism Questions

1. What is your approach to community outreach and evangelism?
2. How do you train and equip the congregation for evangelism?
3. Describe a successful outreach program you have implemented in the past.

4. How do you balance evangelism and discipleship in your ministry?
5. What strategies do you use to engage with the unchurched or non-believers?
6. How do you measure the effectiveness of outreach and evangelism efforts?
7. What role do you believe social justice plays in the church's outreach?

Pastoral Care Questions

1. How do you approach pastoral counseling and care?
2. Describe a time when you helped someone through a significant personal crisis.
3. How do you ensure that pastoral care is a shared responsibility among church staff and leaders?
4. What is your approach to hospital visits and caring for the sick?
5. How do you minister to those who are grieving or going through difficult times?
6. How do you handle confidentiality and sensitive issues in pastoral care?
7. How do you ensure you are accessible to your congregation while maintaining healthy boundaries?

Developing Vision and Ministry Questions

1. How do you discern and develop a vision for the church?
2. What steps do you take to communicate and implement that vision?
3. How do you involve the congregation in the visioning process?
4. Describe a time when you successfully led a church through a significant change or transition.
5. How do you prioritize and set goals for ministry initiatives?
6. What role does strategic planning play in your ministry approach?
7. How do you measure the success of ministry programs and initiatives?
8. How do you develop and mentor other leaders within the church?
9. How do you stay adaptable and open to new ministry opportunities?
10. What is your approach to intergenerational ministry?
11. How do you incorporate feedback from the congregation into your vision and planning?

12. Describe a time when you faced opposition to your vision and how you handled it.

Leadership Style Questions

1. How would you describe your leadership style?
2. How do you build and maintain a strong team of staff and volunteers?
3. What is your approach to conflict resolution within the church?
4. How do you handle criticism or differing opinions from church members?
5. Describe a time when you had to make a difficult leadership decision.
6. How do you ensure clear and effective communication within the church?
7. How do you foster a culture of collaboration and unity in the church?

Pastor and Family Questions

1. How does your family feel about your calling to ministry?
2. How do you balance the demands of ministry with your family life?
3. What role does your family play in your ministry?
4. How do you protect your family's privacy and time from ministry demands?
5. Describe how you involve your family in the life of the church.
6. How do you handle family conflicts or challenges in relation to your pastoral role?
7. How do you ensure that your family feels supported by the church community?
8. What are your expectations for the church's support of your family?
9. How do you communicate with your family about ministry-related stress and challenges?
10. How does your family participate in your spiritual life and disciplines?
11. How do you handle time management to ensure quality time with your family?
12. What are your family's expectations for their involvement in church activities?

Spouse-Related Questions

1. How does your spouse feel about your potential role as the lead pastor of our church?
2. What role does your spouse expect to play in the church community?

3. How do you and your spouse support each other's spiritual growth and ministry?
4. How does your spouse handle the pressures and expectations of pastoral ministry?
5. What boundaries do you and your spouse set to protect your family time?
6. How do you ensure your spouse feels valued and included in the church community?
7. What are your spouse's strengths and interests in relation to church involvement?

These questions cover a broad range of topics and will help provide a comprehensive understanding of each candidate's suitability for the role of Lead Pastor.

The In-Depth Interview

Conducting In-Depth Interviews

Once the committee has selected candidates who have successfully surpassed the qualifications and initial interview, a comprehensive interview should follow. This interview may utilize sample questions from this section, but should include discussions on theology, pastoral care and leadership style. The best questions should include feedback from the initial interview, application and/or resume, books or articles the pastor has written, and sermons they have preached. In-depth interviews should also include the strengths, weaknesses, opportunities, and threats the pastor has navigated and setbacks that they have endured, highlighting their resiliency.

There are two considerations that should precede the in-depth interview:

1. **Assessing Preaching Skills and Pastoral Care:** Request sample sermons and conduct simulated pastoral care scenarios, if possible.

2. **Visiting Current Church** (if applicable): If appropriate, visit the candidate's current church to observe their ministry firsthand.

Comprehensive In-Depth Interview Questions for Lead Pastor Candidates

Theology

1. **Theological Foundations**
   o Can you describe your theological journey and how it has shaped your current beliefs?
   o How do you ensure that your preaching and teaching remain biblically sound and theologically accurate?

2. **Doctrinal Beliefs**
   - o What are your views on the authority of Scripture?
   - o How do you approach complex or controversial theological issues within the church?
   - o What is your understanding of the Trinity and how do you communicate this doctrine to your congregation?

3. **Salvation and Grace**
   - o How do you explain the concept of salvation and grace to new believers?
   - o What is your stance on the balance between grace and works in the Christian life?

4. **Sacraments and Ordinances**
   - o What are your views on baptism and the Lord's Supper, and how do you practice these ordinances in your ministry?
   - o How do you prepare congregants for these significant events?

5. **Spiritual Gifts and the Holy Spirit**
   - o How do you understand and teach the role of the Holy Spirit in the life of a believer?
   - o How do you help members of your congregation discover and use their spiritual gifts?

6. **End Times and Eschatology**
   - o What is your perspective on eschatology (end times theology)?
   - o How do you teach about the end times in a way that is biblically grounded and not sensationalist?

Pastoral Care

1. **Personal Pastoral Care**
   - o Can you describe your approach to pastoral care and counseling?
   - o How do you balance your time between administrative duties and pastoral care?

2. **Crisis and Grief Counseling**
   - How do you provide support to individuals and families during times of crisis or grief?
   - Can you share an example of a time you helped someone through a difficult situation?

3. **Hospital and Home Visits**
   - How do you prioritize and manage hospital and home visits within a large congregation?
   - How do you ensure that no member feels neglected?

4. **Marriage and Family Counseling**
   - What is your approach to marriage and family counseling within the church?
   - How do you address marital issues and support families in your congregation?

5. **Confidentiality and Trust**
   - How do you maintain confidentiality and build trust with your congregants?
   - Can you share how you handle sensitive information?

6. **Conflict Resolution**
   - How do you handle conflicts within the church, whether between members or staff?
   - Can you provide an example of a conflict you resolved and the steps you took?

Leadership Style

1. **Vision and Strategic Planning**
   - How do you develop and communicate a vision for the church?
   - Can you describe a time when you successfully implemented a strategic plan?

2. **Team Leadership and Development**
   - How do you build and lead a cohesive team of church staff and volunteers?
   - What is your approach to mentoring and developing other leaders within the church?

3. **Decision Making and Delegation**
   - How do you approach decision making in a leadership role?
   - How do you determine which tasks to delegate and to whom?

4. **Communication Skills**
   o How do you ensure effective communication within the church, especially in a large congregation?
   o Can you provide examples of how you have effectively communicated important changes or initiatives?

5. **Adaptability and Change Management**
   o How do you handle change within the church, especially when it involves significant transitions?
   o Can you share a time when you led your church through a period of change and how you managed it?

6. **Community Engagement and Outreach**
   o How do you foster a culture of outreach and community engagement within the church?
   o What strategies have you used to engage with the local community and build relationships?

7. **Financial Oversight and Stewardship**
   o What is your philosophy on church finances and stewardship?
   o How do you ensure financial transparency and integrity within the church?

8. **Work-Life Balance**
   o How do you maintain a healthy work-life balance while fulfilling the demanding role of a lead pastor?
   o What practices do you have in place to ensure your own spiritual and emotional health?

9. **Innovation and Creativity**
   o How do you foster innovation and creativity in church programs and ministries?
   o Can you provide an example of a creative initiative you implemented in your previous ministry?

10. **Diversity**
    o How do you ensure that the church is diverse and welcoming to people of all backgrounds?

- What initiatives have you taken to promote diversity within the church community?

11. Evaluation and Feedback

- How do you assess the effectiveness of church programs and ministries?
- How do you receive and incorporate feedback from the congregation and staff?

12. Spiritual Leadership

- How do you nurture your own spiritual growth and ensure you are leading from a place of spiritual health?
- What spiritual disciplines do you practice regularly, and how do they influence your ministry?

13. Home Life
- How do you maintain a healthy home/work balance?
- How does your spouse compliment your ministry?

These questions are designed to provide a comprehensive understanding of the candidate's theology, pastoral care approach, and leadership style, ensuring they align with the needs and vision of a large congregation.

Phase Six: Final Selection

Committee Deliberation and Decision-Making

Introduction

The search committee now has a great deal of information regarding the short-listed candidates. In fact, the information gleaned from resumes, interviews, references, sermons, and more should provide a clear picture of the candidates from which to make a decision.

Now is the time to select a candidate!

Deliberation and Decision-Making Process for Lead Pastor Candidate

Selecting the right lead pastor for a large church is a critical decision that requires careful deliberation, prayerful discernment, and a structured decision-making process. This document outlines the steps and considerations for the pastoral search committee to follow as they evaluate and decide on the final candidate. The church constitution and bylaws may require a different format that outlined here, so default to the process outlined in your church policies.

Candidate Evaluation

1. **Review Comprehensive Candidate Profiles:** Ensure that all members of the search committee have access to comprehensive profiles of the final candidates,

including their resumes, application materials, interview notes, reference checks, and any other relevant information gathered during the screening process.

2. **Assess Alignment with Church Needs:** Evaluate how each candidate aligns with the specific needs and priorities of the church, considering factors such as leadership style, preaching abilities, vision for ministry, and cultural fit.

3. **Identify Strengths and Areas for Growth:** Discuss the strengths and potential areas for growth or development for each candidate and consider how these might impact their ability to lead the church effectively.

Deliberation and Discernment

1. **Prayerful Reflection:** Encourage each committee member to spend time in individual prayer and reflection, seeking God's wisdom and guidance in discerning the right candidate for the church.

2. **Committee Discussion:** Facilitate open and respectful discussions within the committee, allowing members to share their perspectives, concerns, and insights about each candidate.

3. **Seek Counsel:** If needed, seek counsel from trusted advisors, such as denominational leaders, experienced pastors, or ministry consultants, to gain additional insights and perspectives.

4. **Consensus Building:** Work towards building consensus among the committee members, addressing any concerns or objections raised, and ensuring that the decision is made with unity and a shared commitment to the church's best interests. It might be helpful if the committee seeks unity on the final candidate prior to moving forward.

Decision-Making

1. **Establish Decision Criteria:** Clearly define the criteria and decision-making process for selecting the final candidate, ensuring alignment with the church's bylaws, policies, and governance structure.

2. **Voting Procedures for the search committee:** Determine the voting procedures, such as whether a simple majority or a higher threshold (e.g., two-thirds majority) is required for the final decision from the committee.

3. **Confidentiality and Discretion:** Maintain strict confidentiality throughout the decision-making process, ensuring that sensitive information and deliberations are not shared outside the committee until the final decision is announced.

4. **Communicate the Decision:** Once the decision is made, communicate the selection of the new lead pastor candidate to the board for approval, and once approved, contact the lead pastor candidate to invite them to an official candidate weekened. Once they agree to the weekend, the search committee should notify the congregation in a timely and respectful manner, highlighting the candidate's qualifications and the reasons for their selection.

5. **Offer and Negotiation:** With board approval, extend the official offer to the selected candidate to be presented to the church for a congregational vote. At this point, it would be wise to engage in any necessary negotiations regarding compensation, benefits, and other terms of employment. If a Memorandum of Understanding (MOU) precedes a congregational vote, the MOU should clearly state that it is null and void without a favorable congregational vote. An attorney should create the proper documents to protect the church and candidate. The salary expectations should be included in this document.

Throughout this process, it is essential to maintain a spirit of unity, humility, and a commitment to seeking God's will for the church. The search committee should approach their deliberations and decision-making with prayer, wisdom, and a deep sense of responsibility, recognizing the profound impact that the new lead pastor will have on the spiritual life and direction of the church.

Presenting the Final Candidate to the Church

The day has finally arrived to present the candidate to the church. Once the search committee has recommended a candidate, the church leadership has approved it, and the candidate has agreed to the terms of the MOU, the next step is to present the candidate to the congregation. If required by the church bylaws, the presentation is for membership approval.

Congregational Approval Process

Present the final candidate to the congregation and conduct a vote if required by church bylaws following a comprehensive pastoral candidate weekend.

Comprehensive Pastoral Candidate Weekend

After a thorough search process, the pastoral search committee has identified a potential candidate for the lead pastor position. To ensure a smooth and successful transition, it is essential to plan a comprehensive pastoral candidate weekend that allows the congregation to get acquainted with the candidate and provides opportunities for the candidate to experience the church community firsthand. The following outlines the key components and best practices for organizing a stress-free, unity-building weekend.

I. Get-Acquainted Opportunities

A. Formal Meet-and-Greet

- Schedule a formal meet-and-greet event, such as a reception or a Q&A session, where congregants can interact with the candidate in a structured setting.

Separate meet and greet events for ministry leaders and staff would also be beneficial.

- Provide name tags and encourage attendees to introduce themselves and engage in conversation with the candidate.

- Consider having the candidate share their testimony, ministry vision, and background during this event.

B. Informal Social Gatherings

- Arrange informal social gatherings, such as a potluck dinner or a casual coffee hour, to allow congregants to interact with the candidate in a relaxed setting.

- Encourage church leaders, ministry leaders, and key volunteers to attend and engage with the candidate.

- Provide opportunities for the candidate's spouse and family (if applicable) to meet and connect with the church community.

II. Preaching and Teaching Opportunities

A. Sunday Worship Service

- Schedule the candidate to preach during the main Sunday worship service, allowing the congregation to experience their preaching style and biblical teaching.

- Ensure that the candidate is provided with any necessary information about the church's worship style, order of service, and any specific expectations or guidelines.

B. Bible Study or Small Group Session

- Arrange for the candidate to lead a Bible study or small group session, providing an opportunity to observe their teaching abilities and engagement with congregants in a more intimate setting.

- Encourage attendees to participate actively and ask questions during these sessions.

C. Congregational Q&A Session

- Plan a dedicated Q&A session where congregants can submit questions for the candidate in advance or during the event.
- Establish clear guidelines for the Q&A session, such as time limits, respectful conduct, and the types of questions that are appropriate.
- Consider having a moderator or facilitator to manage the session and ensure that it remains focused and constructive.

Best Practices for the Search Committee on the Candidate Weekend

1. **Communication and Coordination:** Maintain clear communication and coordination among the search committee members, church staff, and leadership to ensure a seamless and well-organized weekend.

2. **Hospitality and Welcoming Environment:** Create a warm and welcoming environment for the candidate and their family, ensuring that they feel valued and appreciated throughout their visit.

3. **Logistical Support:** Provide logistical support, such as transportation, accommodation, and meal arrangements, to minimize stress and allow the candidate to focus on connecting with the congregation.

4. **Feedback and Evaluation:** Develop a process for gathering feedback from the congregation and the candidate after the weekend. This feedback can inform the final decision-making process and help identify areas for improvement in future pastoral transitions.

5. **Prayer and Spiritual Guidance:** Encourage the congregation and the search committee to pray for the candidate and the decision-making process, seeking God's guidance and wisdom throughout the weekend.

6. **Unity and Positivity:** Foster an atmosphere of unity and positivity, emphasizing the church's commitment to supporting and embracing the new lead pastor, regardless of individual preferences or opinions.

By carefully planning and executing a comprehensive pastoral candidate weekend, the church can provide a meaningful opportunity for the congregation to connect with the potential lead pastor and for the candidate to experience the church community firsthand. This process can help build unity, foster a smooth transition, and ultimately contribute to the long-term success of the new pastoral leadership.

Final Congregational Approval: Once the final vote is taken, the candidate is selected, and the candidate accepts the position, the onboarding process may begin. Congratulations! The search committee's job is almost complete.

- **Post-Transition Review.** Meet again as a pastoral search committee to review the transition process and identify strengths and areas for improvement for the process.

- **Gathering Feedback from the Congregation:** Collect feedback from the congregation on the transition and the new pastor's integration.

- **Continuous Improvement for Future Transitions:** Document lessons learned and update the transition manual for future pastoral searches.

A Different Outcome

What happens if the candidate fails to receive a favorable vote, or if they change their mind and decide they are no longer interested in the lead pastor position? Changed minds happen, and in pastoral transitions many variables might change what seemed favorable into an unfavorable outcome. In the highly unlikely event of an unfavorable vote, or the candidate changes their mind, the search committee should consider the addendum document, "Steps to Take if a Vote is Unfavorable or Candidate Declines." This document covers both scenarios.

Phase Seven: Transition and Onboarding
Preparing the Congregation for the New Pastor

Introduction

This is an exciting moment for the committee and the church, but it can also be very stressful. The pastoral search committee should be replaced by a transition team, which should mitigate as much stress as possible.

The following steps will provide a stress-free path to onboarding the new pastor:

- Communicate with the congregation about the new pastor and the transition process.

- Clearly state a reasonable and agreeable timeline for the pastor to assume normal duties.

- Communicate the timeline with the congregation, staff, and all stakeholders.

Welcoming the New Pastor

- Plan a welcoming event and introduce the new pastor to the congregation and community. This is a great time to highlight the new direction of the church, and the installation of the new pastor should be posted on social media, advertised, and promoted as an invited event. Work with the new pastor for timelines and consider a "soft event" before inviting the public to a "big event."

- Setting Up the New Pastor for Success

  o Provide resources, support, and orientation to help the new pastor acclimate to their role. An onboarding document follows. Tailor it to your church context.

  o Providing Ongoing Support Offer continuous support and feedback to the new pastor during their initial months.

Onboarding Document for New Lead Pastor

1. Welcome Letter
2. Church Overview
3. Role and Responsibilities
4. Staff and Leadership Team
5. Congregation and Community
6. Church Policies and Procedures
7. Technology and Resources
8. Initial Meetings and Introductions
9. First 90 Days Plan
10. Ongoing Support and Development

---

1. Welcome Letter

Dear [Pastor's Name],

Welcome to [Church Name]!

We are thrilled to have you join our church family as our new Lead Pastor. This document is designed to help you transition smoothly into your new role and provide you with the resources and information you need to succeed.

Warm regards,

[Church Leadership]

2. Church Overview

History and Mission:
- Brief history of the church
- Mission statement
- Core values and beliefs

Vision:
- Short-term and long-term goals
- Key initiatives and programs

Organizational Structure:
- Diagram of church hierarchy
- Key committees and their functions

3. Role and Responsibilities

Key Responsibilities:

Preaching and teaching
- Pastoral care and counseling
- Leadership and vision casting
- Community outreach and engagement
- Administration and management

Weekly Schedule:
- Typical weekly activities and commitments

- Service times and regular meetings

---

4. Staff and Leadership Team

Staff Directory:
- Names, roles, picture of staff member and contact information of all staff members

Leadership Team:
- Names, pictures and roles of church elders/deacons
- Leadership team meeting schedule

Support Staff:
- Administrative and support staff contacts

---

5. Congregation and Community

Demographics:
- Overview of congregation demographics

Key Congregational Groups:
- Children's ministry
- Youth group
- Adult small groups
- Senior ministry
- Other(s)

Community Profile:

- Description of the local community
- Key community partnerships and outreach programs

---

6. Church Policies and Procedures

Employee Handbook:

- Employment policies
- Code of conduct
- Confidentiality agreements

Church Governance:

- Church bylaws
- Decision-making processes

Safety and Security:

- Child protection policies
- Emergency procedures

---

7. Technology and Resources

Office Setup:

- Office location and setup information
- Key access and security

Technology:

- Church management software
- Email and communication tools
- IT support contact information
- Passwords

Resources:

- Access to church library and study materials
- List of essential church documents

---

8. Initial Meetings and Introductions

Meetings to Schedule:

- One-on-one with key staff members
- Meeting with church elders/deacons
- Introduction to ministry leaders

Introduction to Congregation:

- Plan for introducing the new pastor during services
- Special welcome events (dinners, desserts, picnic, first Sunday, etc.)

---

9. First 90 Days Plan

First Month:

- Focus on getting to know the staff and congregation
- Attend key church events and programs
- Begin familiarizing with church operations and policies

Second Month:

- Start leading regular services and preaching
- Conduct listening sessions with different ministry groups
- Participate in community outreach activities

Third Month:

- Set initial goals and priorities with leadership team
- Review and provide feedback on current programs
- Plan and begin implementing new initiatives

10. Ongoing Support and Development

Mentorship:

- Assign a mentor from the leadership team for guidance and support

Performance Reviews:

- Schedule regular check-ins and performance reviews
- Establish clear goals and expectations

Professional Development:

- Opportunities for conferences, workshops, and continued education
- Budget for professional development activities

Notes:

Keep this document accessible for reference as you settle into your new role.

Do not hesitate to reach out to any staff or leadership team members for additional support.

We are excited for the journey ahead and look forward to working with you to fulfill our mission and vision.

Welcome to [Church Name]!

Addendum

Non-Disclosure Agreement (NDA) for Search Committee Members

This Non-Disclosure Agreement ("Agreement") is made and entered into as of [Date] by and between [Church Name] ("Church"), located at [Church Address], and [Committee Member Name] ("Member"), a member of the Pastoral Search Committee.

Purpose: The purpose of this Agreement is to ensure the confidentiality of all information related to the pastoral search process and to protect the privacy of all candidates involved.

1. Definition of Confidential Information: Confidential Information includes, but is not limited to, candidate applications, resumes, cover letters, references, interviews, communications, deliberations, and any other information disclosed during the search process that is not publicly available.

2. Obligations of the Member: The Member agrees to: a. Keep all Confidential Information strictly confidential. b. Use the Confidential Information solely for the purpose of the pastoral search process. c. Refrain from disclosing Confidential Information to any third party without the prior written consent of the Church. d. Take all necessary precautions to prevent unauthorized access to Confidential Information.

3. Permitted Disclosures: Confidential Information may be disclosed to other members of the Pastoral Search Committee and authorized church personnel who need to know the information to perform their duties, provided they are also bound by confidentiality obligations.

4. Return or Destruction of Confidential Information: Upon completion of the pastoral search process or at the request of the Church, the Member agrees to return or destroy all Confidential Information in their possession, including any copies, notes, or other materials derived from or containing Confidential Information.

5. Term: The obligations of this Agreement shall continue in effect indefinitely, even after the Member is no longer part of the Pastoral Search Committee.

6. Remedies: The Member acknowledges that any breach of this Agreement may cause irreparable harm to the Church and agrees that the Church shall be entitled to seek injunctive relief in addition to any other legal or equitable remedies.

7. Governing Law: This Agreement shall be governed by and construed in accordance with the laws of the state of [State], without regard to its conflict of law principles.

8. Entire Agreement: This Agreement constitutes the entire agreement between the parties with respect to the subject matter hereof and supersedes all prior agreements and understandings, whether written or oral, relating to such subject matter.

9. Amendments: Any amendments or modifications to this Agreement must be made in writing and signed by both parties.

10. Severability: If any provision of this Agreement is found to be unenforceable or invalid, the remaining provisions shall remain in full force and effect.

IN WITNESS WHEREOF, the parties hereto have executed this Non-Disclosure Agreement as of the day and year first above written.

[Church Name]

By: _____ Name: _____ Title: _____

[Committee Member Name]

By: _____ Name: _____

Title: Pastoral Search Committee Member

Date: _____

This Non-Disclosure Agreement ensures that all members of the Pastoral Search Committee understand the importance of confidentiality and are committed to protecting the privacy of all candidates throughout the search process.

Lead Pastor Resume Review Guide

Introduction

This document provides a comprehensive framework for reviewing resumes for the position of Lead Pastor at [Church Name]. It ensures a thorough and consistent evaluation process, helping the search committee identify candidates who meet the church's needs and align with its mission and values.

---

1. Basic Information

Personal Details:

- Name
- Contact Information (Phone, Email)
- Current Address

Professional Summary:

- Brief overview of the candidate's qualifications, experience, and ministry philosophy.

---

2. Educational Background

Theological Education:

- Degrees obtained (Bachelor's, Master's, Doctorate)
- Institutions attended
- Dates of attendance
- Specializations or concentrations

Continuing Education:

- Additional courses, certifications, or workshops attended
- Relevant professional development activities

---

3. Ministry Experience

Pastoral Roles:

- Title and role in each position held
- Name and location of each church or organization
- Dates of employment
- Key responsibilities and accomplishments

Preaching and Teaching:

- Experience in sermon preparation and delivery
- Teaching roles in Bible studies, Sunday school, or other educational programs
- Examples of sermon series or notable teaching topics

---

4. Leadership and Administrative Experience

Leadership Roles:

- Positions of leadership held within the church (e.g., Senior Pastor, Associate Pastor, Ministry Leader)
- Scope of leadership (size of congregation, number of staff supervised)
- Examples of leadership initiatives or programs developed

Administrative Skills:

- Experience in church administration (budget management, strategic planning, church operations)
- Familiarity with church management software and tools
- Examples of successful administrative projects

---

5. Pastoral Care and Counseling

Pastoral Care Experience:

- Experience in providing pastoral care and counseling
- Specific areas of pastoral care (e.g., marriage counseling, grief support, crisis intervention)
- Notable achievements in pastoral care ministry

Counseling Skills:

- Formal training or certifications in counseling
- Examples of counseling situations handled

---

6. Vision and Strategic Planning

Vision Casting:

- Experience in developing and communicating a vision for the church
- Examples of vision implementation and results
- Alignment of vision with the church's mission and values

Strategic Planning:

- Experience in long-term and short-term planning for church growth and development
- Examples of successful strategic initiatives

---

7. Community Engagement

Outreach and Evangelism:

- Experience in leading community outreach programs
- Examples of successful evangelism efforts
- Engagement with local community organizations and leaders

Social Responsibility:

- Involvement in community initiatives
- Examples of community service projects

8. Doctrinal Alignment

Theological Beliefs:

- Statement of faith or doctrinal beliefs
- Alignment with the church's theological positions
- Any areas of potential doctrinal concern

Teaching and Preaching Philosophy:

- Approach to preaching and teaching
- Examples of theological topics covered

9. Personal Qualities and Skills

Personal Characteristics:

- Integrity and character
- Passion for ministry
- Emotional intelligence and interpersonal skills

Additional Skills:

- Technological proficiency
- Multilingual abilities
- Other relevant skills

10. References and Recommendations

Professional References:

- Names and contact information of references

- Relationship to the candidate
- Summary of reference feedback (attach detailed reports)

Letters of Recommendation:

- Include any letters of recommendation provided by the candidate

11. Evaluation Summary

Strengths:

- List of the candidate's key strengths based on the resume review

Areas for Improvement:

- List of potential areas for growth or concerns

Overall Fit:

- Assessment of the candidate's overall fit with the church's needs and culture

Recommendation:

- Initial recommendation for further consideration, interview, or no further action

12. Attachments

Candidate's Resume

- Reference Reports
- Letters of Recommendation
- Additional Supporting Documents

Prepared By:

Name:

Title:

Date:

Search Committee Signatures:

[Signature Line]

[Signature Line]

[Signature Line]

[Signature Line]

[Signature Line]

This guide ensures a comprehensive and consistent review of each candidate's resume, helping the search committee make informed decisions throughout the pastoral search process.

21-Day Devotional, Prayer, Fasting, and Praise Guide for Our Church

Introduction

This 21-day guide is designed to support our Church through its pastoral transition. Each day includes a devotional thought, key scripture, prayer focus, and praise section. As the leaders of the church seek God's guidance, we will commit to prayer, fasting, and praising God for His faithfulness. All Scripture verses in this 21-Day Devotional are from the New International Version.

Day 1: Trust in God's Plan

Scripture: Proverbs 3:5-6

"Trust in the Lord with all your heart and lean not on your own understanding; in all your ways submit to him, and he will make your paths straight."

Devotional Thought: Trusting in God's sovereignty and timing is crucial during this transition. He knows the plans He has for Our Church.

Prayer Focus:

- Pray for the search committee to trust God's guidance.
- Ask for wisdom and discernment for all involved in the search process.

Praise:

Thank God for His faithfulness and trustworthiness in guiding our church through past transitions.

Day 2: Unity and Harmony

Scripture: Ephesians 4:3

"Make every effort to keep the unity of the Spirit through the bond of peace."

Devotional Thought: Unity is essential during this time of change. Let's strive to maintain peace and harmony within our congregation.

Prayer Focus:

- Pray for unity and harmony among church members and leaders.
- Ask God to guard against division and promote understanding.

Praise:

Praise God for the unity He has provided in the past and the peace that surpasses all understanding.

Day 3: Wisdom and Discernment

Scripture: James 1:5

"If any of you lacks wisdom, you should ask God, who gives generously to all without finding fault, and it will be given to you."

Devotional Thought: The search committee has a significant responsibility. Let's ask God to grant them the wisdom they need.

Prayer Focus:

- Pray for wisdom, discernment, and unity for the search committee.
- Ask God to guide their discussions and decisions.

Praise:

Thank God for His promise to give wisdom generously to those who ask.

Day 4: Patience and Peace

Scripture: Philippians 4:6-7

"Do not be anxious about anything, but in every situation, by prayer and petition, with thanksgiving, present your requests to God. And the peace of God, which transcends all understanding, will guard your hearts and your minds in Christ Jesus."

Devotional Thought: Cultivating patience and peace during the waiting period is crucial. God's peace will guard our hearts.

Prayer Focus:

- Pray for patience and peace for the congregation and leadership.
- Ask God to ease any anxieties or concerns.

Praise:

Praise God for His peace that guards our hearts and minds in Christ Jesus.

Day 5: Continued Ministry and Outreach

Scripture: Philippians 1:6

"Being confident of this, that he who began a good work in you will carry it on to completion until the day of Christ Jesus."

Devotional Thought: God is faithful to complete the work He has started in our church. Let's trust Him for the continued ministry.

Prayer Focus:

- Pray for the ongoing ministries and outreach efforts of the church.
- Ask God to bless and sustain all ministry leaders and volunteers.

Praise:

Thank God for His continued work and faithfulness in the ministries of Our Church.

Day 6: Protection from Division

Scripture: 1 Corinthians 1:10

"I appeal to you, brothers and sisters, in the name of our Lord Jesus Christ, that all of you agree with one another in what you say and that there be no divisions among you, but that you be perfectly united in mind and thought."

Devotional Thought: Guarding against division and conflict is essential for unity and progress.

Prayer Focus:

- Pray for protection against division and conflict within the church.
- Ask God to promote understanding and unity.

Praise:

Praise God for the unity and peace He has provided in our church.

Day 7: Encouragement and Support

Scripture: 1 Thessalonians 5:11

"Therefore encourage one another and build each other up, just as in fact you are doing."

Devotional Thought: Providing encouragement and support to each other is crucial during this time.

Prayer Focus:

- Pray for encouragement and support for church members and leaders.
- Ask God to strengthen and uplift those feeling weary or discouraged.

Praise:

Thank God for the ways He has encouraged and built up the church through His people.

Day 8: Financial Stability

Scripture: Philippians 4:19

"And my God will meet all your needs according to the riches of his glory in Christ Jesus."

Devotional Thought: Trusting God to provide for the financial needs of the church during this transition.

Prayer Focus:

- Pray for the financial stability and stewardship of the church's resources.
- Ask God to provide for all the church's needs.

Praise:

Praise God for His abundant provision and faithfulness in meeting the church's financial needs.

Day 9: Preparation for the New Pastor

Scripture: Jeremiah 29:11

"For I know the plans I have for you," declares the Lord, "plans to prosper you and not to harm you, plans to give you hope and a future."

Devotional Thought: God has already planned the next chapter for our church and our future pastor.

Prayer Focus:

- Pray for the future lead pastor, that God would prepare their heart and mind for this calling.
- Ask God to give them peace and clarity as they consider this position.

Praise:

Thank God for His good plans and the future He has in store for our church and new pastor.

Day 10: Faithfulness in Prayer

Scripture: 1 Thessalonians 5:16-18

"Rejoice always, pray continually, give thanks in all circumstances; for this is God's will for you in Christ Jesus."

Devotional Thought: Encouraging a strong, consistent prayer life within the church is vital.

Prayer Focus:

- Pray for a spirit of prayer and faithfulness within the church.
- Ask God to deepen the prayer lives of all members.

Praise:
Praise God for the power of prayer and His faithfulness in answering.

Day 11: God's Direction for the Search Committee

Scripture: Psalm 25:4-5
"Show me your ways, Lord, teach me your paths. Guide me in your truth and teach me, for you are God my Savior, and my hope is in you all day long."

Devotional Thought: Seeking God's direction for the search committee in identifying and selecting the right candidate.

Prayer Focus:

- Pray for clear direction and guidance for the search committee.
- Ask God to reveal His will and lead them to the right candidate.

Praise:
Thank God for His promise to guide and teach us His ways.

Day 12: Spiritual Growth

Scripture: Colossians 1:9-10
"For this reason, since the day we heard about you, we have not stopped praying for you. We continually ask God to fill you with the knowledge of his will through all the wisdom and understanding that the Spirit gives, so that you may live a life worthy of the Lord and please him in every way: bearing fruit in every good work, growing in the knowledge of God."

Devotional Thought: Praying for the spiritual growth and deepening faith of the congregation.

Prayer Focus:
- Pray for spiritual growth and maturity among church members.
- Ask God to fill the congregation with His wisdom and understanding.

Praise:

Praise God for the spiritual growth and fruit He is producing in our lives.

Day 13: Outreach to the Lost

Scripture: Matthew 28:19-20

"Therefore go and make disciples of all nations, baptizing them in the name of the Father and of the Son and of the Holy Spirit, and teaching them to obey everything I have commanded you. And surely I am with you always, to the very end of the age."

Devotional Thought: Keeping a focus on evangelism and outreach to the lost in the community.

Prayer Focus:
- Pray for opportunities to reach the lost in our community.
- Ask God to give us boldness and compassion to share the Gospel.

Praise:

Thank God for His promise to be with us as we make disciples.

Day 14: Support for Interim Leaders

Scripture: Hebrews 13:7

"Remember your leaders, who spoke the word of God to you. Consider the outcome of their way of life and imitate their faith."

Devotional Thought: Supporting interim leaders and those stepping up during the transition period.

Prayer Focus:

- Pray for strength, wisdom, and encouragement for interim leaders.
- Ask God to bless their efforts and guide their leadership.

Praise:

Thank God for providing leaders to guide us during this transition.

Day 15: Gratitude for the Past

Scripture: 1 Chronicles 16:34

"Give thanks to the Lord, for he is good; his love endures forever."

Devotional Thought: Expressing gratitude for the previous pastor's ministry and the church's history.

Prayer Focus:

- Pray a prayer of thanks for the past leadership and their contributions.
- Ask God to bless the previous pastor and his family in their next chapter.

Praise:

Praise God for His goodness and enduring love throughout our church's history.

Day 16: Trust in God's Timing

Scripture: Ecclesiastes 3:1

"There is a time for everything, and a season for every activity under the heavens."

Devotional Thought: Trusting in God's perfect timing for every step of the search process.

Prayer Focus:

- Pray for patience and trust in God's timing.
- Ask God to orchestrate every detail according to His perfect plan.

Praise:

Thank God for His perfect timing and His control over every season.

Day 17: Praying for the Candidate's Family

Scripture: Joshua 24:15

"But as for me and my household, we will serve the Lord."

Devotional Thought: The candidate's family is an integral part of the pastoral transition.

Prayer Focus:

- Pray for the family of the future lead pastor, for their unity and support.
- Ask God to prepare their hearts for the transition and new beginnings.

Praise:

Thank God for the blessing of family and their role in ministry.

Day 18: Praying for Church Finances

Scripture: Malachi 3:10

"Bring the whole tithe into the storehouse, that there may be food in my house. Test me in this," says the Lord Almighty, "and see if I will not throw open the floodgates of heaven and pour out so much blessing that there will not be room enough to store it."

Devotional Thought: Trusting God to provide financially for the church during this transition.

Prayer Focus:
- Pray for the financial stability and growth of the church.
- Ask God to bless the church's stewardship and generosity.

Praise:

Praise God for His abundant provision and the blessings He has poured out.

Day 19: Encouragement for the Congregation

Scripture: Hebrews 10:24-25

"And let us consider how we may spur one another on toward love and good deeds, not giving up meeting together, as some are in the habit of doing, but encouraging one another—and all the more as you see the Day approaching."

Devotional Thought: Encouraging one another during this time of change.

Prayer Focus:
- Pray for encouragement and strength for each member of the congregation.
- Ask God to build up the church's faith and hope.

Praise:
Thank God for the community of believers and the encouragement we receive from each other.

Day 20: Praying for God's Will to Be Done

Scripture: Matthew 6:10
"Your kingdom come, your will be done, on earth as it is in heaven."

Devotional Thought: Seeking God's will above all else in the search process.

Prayer Focus:
- Pray for God's will to be done in every aspect of the pastoral search.
- Ask God to align the hearts and minds of all involved with His purpose.

Praise:
Praise God for His perfect will and His plan for our church.

Day 21: Giving Thanks and Trusting God

Scripture: 1 Thessalonians 5:16-18
"Rejoice always, pray continually, give thanks in all circumstances; for this is God's will for you in Christ Jesus."

Devotional Thought: Giving thanks to God for His faithfulness throughout the transition process.

Prayer Focus:

- Thank God for His guidance, provision, and faithfulness.
- Pray for continued trust and faith in God's plan for the church's future.

Praise:

Thank God for His faithfulness and rejoice in His goodness and mercy.

As we conclude this 21-day devotional, prayer, fasting, and praise guide, let us remain steadfast in seeking God, trusting His plan, and giving Him all the glory. May He lead our church to a future filled with hope, purpose, and unity.

Job Description for Lead Pastor (under 125 members)

- **Position Title:** Lead Pastor
- **Church Name:** [Church Name]
- **Location:** [City, State]
- **Reports To:** Church Board
- **Position Type:** Full-Time/Part-Time

Position Summary

[Church Name] is seeking a compassionate, spiritually mature, and dedicated Lead Pastor to provide leadership and guidance to our congregation of under 125 members. The Lead Pastor will be responsible for preaching, teaching, pastoral care, and overall spiritual leadership. This individual will work collaboratively with the church board and volunteers to fulfill the church's mission and vision.

Key Responsibilities

Preaching and Teaching

- Prepare and deliver weekly sermons that are biblically sound, relevant, and inspiring.
- Lead and teach Bible studies, Sunday school classes, and other educational programs.
- Encourage and develop lay leaders and teachers within the congregation.

Pastoral Care

- Provide pastoral care and counseling to members, including hospital visits, home visits, and crisis intervention.
- Officiate weddings, funerals, baptisms, and other church ceremonies.
- Support and nurture the spiritual well-being of the congregation.

Leadership and Administration

- Collaborate with the church board to set and implement the church's vision, mission, and strategic goals.
- Oversee the church's ministries, programs, and activities, ensuring alignment with the church's mission.
- Manage the church's administrative functions, including budgeting, financial oversight, and facility management.
- Lead and mentor church staff and volunteers, fostering a positive and collaborative working environment.

Community Outreach and Engagement

- Promote and participate in community outreach initiatives to grow the church's presence and impact.
- Build relationships with local organizations, other churches, and community leaders.
- Encourage the congregation to engage in evangelism and service opportunities.

Personal and Professional Development

- Maintain a personal life of prayer, study, and spiritual growth.
- Pursue continuing education and professional development opportunities to enhance pastoral skills.

Qualifications

- A committed follower of Jesus Christ with a deep personal relationship with God.
- Ordained or eligible for ordination within [Denomination] (if applicable).
- Minimum of a Bachelor's degree in Theology, Divinity, or a related field (Master's degree preferred).
- Previous pastoral experience, preferably in a small church setting.
- Strong biblical knowledge and ability to communicate scriptural truths effectively.
- Excellent interpersonal and communication skills.
- Ability to lead, inspire, and work collaboratively with others.

- Demonstrated ability to manage administrative and financial responsibilities.
- Commitment to the vision, mission, and values of [Church Name].

Expectations

- Exhibit a Christ-like character and model a life of faith, integrity, and humility.
- Be accessible and approachable to all church members.
- Demonstrate flexibility and adaptability in responding to the needs of the congregation.
- Engage actively in the life of the church and its community.
- Respect and appreciate the traditions and history of [Church Name] while leading towards growth and change.
- Maintain confidentiality and exhibit discretion in handling sensitive information.
- Participate in regular performance evaluations with the church board.

Application Process

Interested candidates should submit the following:

- A cover letter expressing their interest in the position and alignment with the church's mission.
- A current resume or CV detailing their educational background, ministry experience, and relevant skills.
- A statement of faith and philosophy of ministry.
- Contact information for at least three professional references.

Please send application materials to [Contact Person] at [Email Address] or [Mailing Address] by [Application Deadline].

Conclusion

[Church Name] is excited to welcome a new Lead Pastor who will help us grow in our faith and reach our community with the love of Christ. We look forward to discerning God's will together in this important transition.

This job description outlines the primary duties and expectations for the Lead Pastor role at [Church Name]. The responsibilities and qualifications listed are not exhaustive, and additional tasks may be assigned as needed.

Job Description for Lead Pastor (Medium Church)

- **Position Title:** Lead Pastor
- **Church Name:** [Church Name]
- **Location:** [City, State]
- **Reports To:** Church Board
- **Position Type:** Full-Time

Position Summary

[Church Name] is seeking a dynamic, spiritually mature, and visionary Lead Pastor to provide leadership and direction for our congregation of under 500 members. The Lead Pastor will be responsible for preaching, teaching, pastoral care, and overall spiritual leadership. This individual will work collaboratively with the church board, staff, and volunteers to fulfill the church's mission and vision.

Key Responsibilities

Preaching and Teaching

- Prepare and deliver weekly sermons that are biblically sound, relevant, and inspiring.
- Lead and teach Bible studies, Sunday school classes, and other educational programs.
- Encourage and develop lay leaders and teachers within the congregation.

Pastoral Care

- Provide pastoral care and counseling to members, including hospital visits, home visits, and crisis intervention.
- Officiate weddings, funerals, baptisms, and other church ceremonies.
- Support and nurture the spiritual well-being of the congregation.

Leadership and Administration

- Collaborate with the church board to set and implement the church's vision, mission, and strategic goals.

- Oversee the church's ministries, programs, and activities, ensuring alignment with the church's mission.
- Manage the church's administrative functions, including budgeting, financial oversight, and facility management.
- Lead and mentor church staff and volunteers, fostering a positive and collaborative working environment.

Community Outreach and Engagement

- Promote and participate in community outreach initiatives to grow the church's presence and impact.
- Build relationships with local organizations, other churches, and community leaders.
- Encourage the congregation to engage in evangelism and service opportunities.

Personal and Professional Development

- Maintain a personal life of prayer, study, and spiritual growth.
- Pursue continuing education and professional development opportunities to enhance pastoral skills.

Additional Responsibilities

- Develop and implement strategies for church growth and member retention.
- Facilitate effective communication within the church and between the church and the community.
- Oversee the use of technology and social media to enhance the church's ministry and outreach efforts.

Qualifications

- A committed follower of Jesus Christ with a deep personal relationship with God.
- Ordained or eligible for ordination within [Denomination] (if applicable).
- Minimum of a Bachelor's degree in Theology, Divinity, or a related field (Master's degree preferred).

- Significant pastoral experience, preferably in a medium-sized church setting.
- Strong biblical knowledge and ability to communicate scriptural truths effectively.
- Excellent interpersonal and communication skills.
- Proven leadership abilities and experience managing church operations.
- Commitment to the vision, mission, and values of [Church Name].

Expectations

- Exhibit a Christ-like character and model a life of faith, integrity, and humility.
- Be accessible and approachable to all church members.
- Demonstrate flexibility and adaptability in responding to the needs of the congregation.
- Engage actively in the life of the church and its community.
- Respect and appreciate the traditions and history of [Church Name] while leading towards growth and change.
- Maintain confidentiality and exhibit discretion in handling sensitive information.
- Participate in regular performance evaluations with the church board.
- Encourage a culture of volunteerism and active participation among church members.
- Be a visible and active presence in the community, representing the church in a positive and impactful manner.

Application Process

Interested candidates should submit the following:

- A cover letter expressing their interest in the position and alignment with the church's mission.
- A current resume or CV detailing their educational background, ministry experience, and relevant skills.
- A statement of faith and philosophy of ministry.
- Contact information for at least three professional references.

Please send application materials to [Contact Person] at [Email Address] or [Mailing Address] by [Application Deadline].

Conclusion

[Church Name] is excited to welcome a new Lead Pastor who will help us grow in our faith and reach our community with the love of Christ. We look forward to discerning God's will together in this important transition.

This job description outlines the primary duties and expectations for the Lead Pastor role at [Church Name]. The responsibilities and qualifications listed are not exhaustive, and additional tasks may be assigned as needed.

Job Description for Lead Pastor (Large Church)

- **Position Title:** Lead Pastor
- **Church Name:** [Church Name]
- **Location:** [City, State]
- **Reports To:** Church Board
- **Position Type:** Full-Time

Position Summary

[Church Name] is seeking an experienced, spiritually mature, and visionary Lead Pastor to provide leadership and direction for our congregation of over 1000 members and more than 12 staff members. The Lead Pastor will be responsible for preaching, teaching, pastoral care, strategic planning, and overall spiritual leadership. This individual will work collaboratively with the church board, staff, and volunteers to fulfill the church's mission and vision and to foster spiritual growth and community engagement.

Key Responsibilities

Preaching and Teaching

- Prepare and deliver weekly sermons that are biblically sound, relevant, and inspiring.
- Oversee the development and delivery of Bible studies, Sunday school classes, and other educational programs.
- Encourage and develop lay leaders and teachers within the congregation.

Pastoral Care

- Provide pastoral care and counseling to members, including hospital visits, home visits, and crisis intervention.
- Officiate weddings, funerals, baptisms, and other church ceremonies.
- Support and nurture the spiritual well-being of the congregation.

Leadership and Administration

- Collaborate with the church board to set and implement the church's vision, mission, and strategic goals.
- Oversee the church's ministries, programs, and activities, ensuring alignment with the church's mission.
- Manage the church's administrative functions, including budgeting, financial oversight, and facility management.
- Lead and mentor church staff and volunteers, fostering a positive and collaborative working environment.
- Ensure effective communication and coordination among the church's various ministries and departments.

Community Outreach and Engagement

- Promote and participate in community outreach initiatives to grow the church's presence and impact.
- Build relationships with local organizations, other churches, and community leaders.
- Encourage the congregation to engage in evangelism and service opportunities.

Strategic Planning and Vision

- Develop and implement strategies for church growth and member retention.
- Facilitate long-term strategic planning initiatives in collaboration with the church board and staff.
- Regularly evaluate and adjust ministry programs to ensure they are meeting the needs of the congregation and community.

Personal and Professional Development

- Maintain a personal life of prayer, study, and spiritual growth.
- Pursue continuing education and professional development opportunities to enhance pastoral skills.

Additional Responsibilities

- Oversee the use of technology and social media to enhance the church's ministry and outreach efforts.
- Represent the church in denominational and community events.
- Lead the church in special projects and initiatives as directed by the church board.

Qualifications

- A committed follower of Jesus Christ with a deep personal relationship with God.
- Ordained or eligible for ordination within [Denomination] (if applicable).
- Minimum of a Master's degree in Theology, Divinity, or a related field (Doctorate preferred).
- Extensive pastoral experience, preferably in a large or mega church setting.
- Strong biblical knowledge and ability to communicate scriptural truths effectively.
- Proven leadership abilities and experience managing large church operations.
- Excellent interpersonal and communication skills.
- Demonstrated ability to develop and implement strategic plans.
- Commitment to the vision, mission, and values of [Church Name].

Expectations

- Exhibit a Christ-like character and model a life of faith, integrity, and humility.
- Be accessible and approachable to all church members.
- Demonstrate flexibility and adaptability in responding to the needs of the congregation.
- Engage actively in the life of the church and its community.
- Respect and appreciate the traditions and history of [Church Name] while leading towards growth and change.
- Maintain confidentiality and exhibit discretion in handling sensitive information.
- Participate in regular performance evaluations with the church board.
- Encourage a culture of volunteerism and active participation among church members.

- Be a visible and active presence in the community, representing the church in a positive and impactful manner.

Application Process

Interested candidates should submit the following:

- A cover letter expressing their interest in the position and alignment with the church's mission.
- A current resume or CV detailing their educational background, ministry experience, and relevant skills.
- A statement of faith and philosophy of ministry.
- Contact information for at least three professional references.

Please send application materials to [Contact Person] at [Email Address] or [Mailing Address] by [Application Deadline].

Conclusion

[Church Name] is excited to welcome a new Lead Pastor who will help us grow in our faith and reach our community with the love of Christ. We look forward to discerning God's will together in this important transition.

This job description outlines the primary duties and expectations for the Lead Pastor role at [Church Name]. The responsibilities and qualifications listed are not exhaustive, and additional tasks may be assigned as needed.

Suggested Questions for the Pastoral Search Committee to Ask References

1. **Professional Background:**

   o   How long have you known the candidate, and in what capacity?

   o   Can you describe the candidate's leadership style?

2. **Pastoral Skills:**

   o   How does the candidate handle preaching and teaching? Are their sermons engaging and theologically sound?

   o   Can you provide an example of how the candidate has successfully led a church through a difficult situation?

3. **Spiritual and Theological Insight:**

   o   How does the candidate demonstrate their commitment to prayer and personal spiritual growth?

   o   How does the candidate approach theological education and continuing development?

4. **Relationship with Congregation:**

   o   How does the candidate build and maintain relationships within the congregation?

   o   Can you give an example of how the candidate has dealt with conflict or disagreements within the church?

5. **Pastoral Care:**

   o   How does the candidate handle pastoral care, such as visiting the sick and counseling members in crisis?

   o   How effective is the candidate in providing spiritual guidance and support to individuals?

6. **Administrative Abilities:**

   o How does the candidate manage their time and prioritize tasks?

   o Can you describe the candidate's approach to delegating responsibilities?

7. **Vision and Planning:**

   o How does the candidate develop and communicate a vision for the church?

   o Can you provide an example of a successful initiative the candidate has led?

8. **Community Engagement:**

   o How does the candidate interact with and impact the local community outside the church?

   o Can you describe the candidate's involvement in community outreach programs?

9. **Team Collaboration:**

   o How does the candidate work with other church staff and volunteers?

   o Can you provide an example of how the candidate has fostered teamwork and collaboration?

10. **Conflict Resolution:**

    o How does the candidate handle conflicts within the church?

    o Can you provide an example of a time when the candidate successfully resolved a significant issue?

11. **Adaptability:**

    o How does the candidate handle change and unexpected challenges?

    o Can you give an example of how the candidate adapted to a major shift within the church or community?

12. **Cultural Sensitivity:**

    o How does the candidate demonstrate cultural awareness and sensitivity?

    o Can you describe a time when the candidate effectively ministered to a diverse congregation?

13. **Ethics and Integrity:**

   o How does the candidate uphold ethical standards and integrity in their ministry?

   o Have you ever observed the candidate in a situation that tested their ethical judgment?

14. **Personal Attributes:**

   o How would you describe the candidate's personality and character?

   o What are the candidate's greatest strengths and areas for improvement?

15. **Impact on Previous Congregation:**

   o How did the candidate's previous congregation respond to their leadership?

   o What notable changes or improvements occurred during the candidate's tenure?

16. **Professional Development:**

   o How does the candidate stay informed about current trends and issues in ministry?

   o Can you provide an example of the candidate pursuing further education or training?

17. **Communication Skills:**

   o How effectively does the candidate communicate with different groups within the church (e.g., youth, elders, committees)?

   o Can you describe a time when the candidate successfully navigated a challenging communication issue?

18. **Vision for Growth:**

   o How does the candidate plan for and implement church growth strategies?

   o Can you provide an example of the candidate leading a successful growth initiative?

19. **Financial Stewardship:**

   o How does the candidate manage church finances and budgetary matters?

   o Can you describe the candidate's approach to financial planning and transparency?

20. **Feedback and Improvement:**

   o How does the candidate receive and respond to constructive feedback?

   o Can you give an example of the candidate making significant improvements based on feedback?

21. **Family and Personal Life:**

   o How does the candidate balance their ministry responsibilities with their family and personal life?

   o Can you describe how the candidate's family supports their ministry?

22. **Mentorship and Discipleship:**

   o How does the candidate mentor and disciple other leaders and members within the church?

   o Can you provide an example of a successful mentorship relationship the candidate has had?

23. **Innovative Practices:**

   o How does the candidate incorporate new and innovative practices into their ministry?

   o Can you describe a time when the candidate successfully implemented a new approach or idea?

24. **Commitment to Mission:**

   o How does the candidate demonstrate their commitment to the church's mission and values?

   o Can you provide an example of the candidate embodying the church's mission in their work?

25. **Overall Assessment:**

   o What is your overall impression of the candidate's suitability for the lead pastor position?

   o Would you recommend the candidate for this role, and why or why not?

Steps to Take If a Vote is Unfavorable or Candidate Declines

Introduction

The process of selecting a new lead pastor is critical and can be challenging, especially if a candidate does not receive a favorable vote from the congregation or changes their mind after a congregational vote. Do not lose heart, however. This document outlines the steps to take in such a scenario, including prayer, reviewing previous shortlisted candidates, and evaluating the weaknesses of the initial candidate.

Step 1: Seek Guidance Through Prayer

Prayer Focus

- **Pray for Wisdom:** Ask God for wisdom and discernment for the search committee and church leadership as they navigate this situation.
- **Pray for Unity:** Pray for unity within the congregation, that members will remain supportive and understanding throughout the process.
- **Pray for the Candidate:** Pray for the candidate, that they will be encouraged and guided in their future ministry.

Scripture for Reflection

- **James 1:5:** "If any of you lacks wisdom, you should ask God, who gives generously to all without finding fault, and it will be given to you."
- **Philippians 4:6-7:** "Do not be anxious about anything, but in every situation, by prayer and petition, with thanksgiving, present your requests to God. And the peace of God, which transcends all understanding, will guard your hearts and your minds in Christ Jesus."

Step 2: Communicate with the Congregation

Transparency and Honesty

- **Inform the Congregation:** Communicate the results of the vote transparently to the congregation. Emphasize the importance of unity and trust in the search process.
- **Provide Reassurance:** Reassure the congregation that the search committee remains committed to finding the right candidate for the church.

Key Points to Include

- **Acknowledgment:** Acknowledge the efforts and qualities of the candidate who did not receive a favorable vote.
- **Next Steps:** Outline the steps the search committee will take moving forward, including prayer, review, and continued search efforts.

Step 3: Review Shortlisted Candidates

Re-evaluate the Shortlist

- **Revisit Previous Candidates:** Review the profiles of previously shortlisted candidates to determine if any of them meet the criteria and needs of the church.
- **New Interviews:** Consider conducting new interviews with the shortlisted candidates to gain fresh insights and perspectives.

Criteria for Review

- **Alignment with Church Mission:** Ensure that candidates align with the church's mission, vision, and values.
- **Feedback from Initial Interviews:** Review feedback and evaluations from the initial interview process.

Step 4: Evaluate the Weaknesses of the Initial Candidate

Detailed Evaluation

- **Identify Weaknesses:** Conduct a thorough evaluation of the reasons why the initial candidate did not receive a favorable vote. This may include feedback from the congregation and the search committee's observations.
- **Constructive Feedback:** Prepare constructive feedback for the candidate to help them in their future endeavors.

Key Areas for Evaluation

- **Theological Alignment:** Ensure that the candidate's theological beliefs align with those of the church.
- **Leadership Style:** Assess whether the candidate's leadership style matches the needs and culture of the congregation.
- **Communication Skills:** Evaluate the effectiveness of the candidate's communication and preaching abilities.
- **Pastoral Care:** Consider the candidate's approach to pastoral care and their ability to connect with the congregation.

Step 5: Continue the Search Process

Renewed Search Efforts

- **Advertise the Position:** Re-advertise the lead pastor position if necessary, using various platforms to attract new candidates.
- **Expand the Search:** Broaden the search to include candidates from different regions or networks.

Maintaining Momentum

- **Regular Updates:** Keep the congregation informed of the search process and progress regularly.
- **Engage the Congregation:** Encourage the congregation to continue praying for the search process and to remain patient and supportive.

Conclusion

Navigating the process when a pastoral candidate does not receive a favorable vote requires prayer, transparency, and strategic planning. By seeking God's guidance, communicating effectively with the congregation, reviewing shortlisted candidates, and evaluating the weaknesses of the initial candidate, the search committee can continue to work towards finding the right lead pastor for the church. Through this process, the church can remain united and focused on its mission and vision.

Lead Pastor Sermon Evaluation Tool

Instructions: Use this tool to evaluate the sermons delivered by pastoral candidates. Rate each category on a scale from 1 (Poor) to 5 (Excellent). Provide comments to support your ratings and offer specific feedback.

Candidate Name: _____ **Date of Sermon:** _____

Evaluator Name: _____

Content and Message

1. **Biblical Accuracy:**
   - **Definition:** The extent to which the sermon correctly interprets and applies Scripture.
   - **Considerations:** Are the Scripture references accurate and contextually appropriate? Is the theological interpretation sound?

   Score: _____

   Comments: _____

   _____

2. **Theological Soundness:**
   - **Definition:** The alignment of the sermon's message with core Christian doctrines and beliefs.
   - **Considerations:** Does the sermon reflect the essential truths of the faith? Is it free from heretical or controversial teachings?

   Score: _____

   Comments: _____

   _____

3. **Clarity and Coherence of Message:**
   - ○ **Definition:** The logical flow and understandability of the sermon.
   - ○ **Considerations:** Is the main point clear and well-articulated? Are the supporting points logically structured and easy to follow?

   Score: _____

   Comments: _____

   _____

4. **Relevance to Congregation:**
   - ○ **Definition:** The applicability of the sermon's message to the congregation's needs and context.
   - ○ **Considerations:** Does the sermon address current issues or concerns within the congregation? Is it culturally and situationally relevant?

   Score: _____

   Comments: _____

   _____

5. **Depth and Insightfulness:**
   - ○ **Definition:** The intellectual and spiritual depth of the sermon.
   - ○ **Considerations:** Does the sermon provide deep insights into the Scripture and its application? Does it challenge the congregation to think and grow spiritually?

   Score: _____

   Comments: _____

   _____

Delivery and Presentation

6. **Engagement with Audience:**
   - ○ **Definition:** The speaker's ability to connect with and hold the attention of the audience.
   - ○ **Considerations:** Does the preacher engage the congregation through eye contact, interaction, and enthusiasm? Is the congregation responsive and attentive?

   Score: ____

   Comments: _____

   _____

7. **Vocal Clarity and Projection:**
   - ○ **Definition:** The clarity, volume, and articulation of the speaker's voice.
   - ○ **Considerations:** Is the preacher's voice clear and easy to understand? Is the volume appropriate for the space? Does the preacher use vocal variety to maintain interest?

   Score: ____

   Comments: _____

   _____

8. **Body Language and Presence:**
   - ○ **Definition:** The effectiveness of the speaker's non-verbal communication.
   - ○ **Considerations:** Does the preacher use appropriate gestures and facial expressions? Is their posture confident and engaging? Does their presence command attention?

   Score: ____

   Comments: _____

   _____

9. **Use of Illustrations and Examples:**
   - ○ **Definition:** The effectiveness of stories, analogies, and examples in enhancing the message.
   - ○ **Considerations:** Are the illustrations relevant and impactful? Do they help clarify and reinforce the sermon's points? Are they culturally and contextually appropriate?

   Score: ____

   Comments: _____

   _____

10. **Pacing and Timing:**
    - ○ **Definition:** The speaker's control over the tempo and duration of the sermon.
    - ○ **Considerations:** Is the sermon well-paced, avoiding rushed or dragging segments? Is the length of the sermon appropriate for the context and audience?

    Score: ____

    Comments: _____

    _____

Spiritual Impact

11. **Inspiration and Motivation:**
    o **Definition:** The sermon's ability to inspire and motivate the congregation spiritually.
    o **Considerations:** Does the sermon move the congregation to deeper faith and action? Does it inspire hope, conviction, and commitment?

    Score: ____

    Comments: _____

    _____

12. **Call to Action/Practical Application:**
    o **Definition:** The clarity and effectiveness of the sermon's practical application and call to action.
    o **Considerations:** Does the sermon offer clear, actionable steps for the congregation? Is there a compelling call to live out the message?

    Score: ____

    Comments: _____

    _____

13. **Sensitivity to the Holy Spirit:**
    - ○ **Definition:** The preacher's awareness and responsiveness to the guidance of the Holy Spirit during the sermon.
    - ○ **Considerations:** Is there evidence that the preacher is led by the Holy Spirit in their delivery and content? Are moments of spiritual significance recognized and appropriately addressed?

    Score: _____

    Comments: _____

    _____

Overall Impressions

14. **Overall Effectiveness of Sermon:**
    - ○ **Definition:** The general impact and effectiveness of the sermon as a whole.
    - ○ **Considerations:** Taking all factors into account, how effective was the sermon in achieving its intended purpose and impact?

    Score: _____

    Comments: _____

    _____

15. **Strengths of the Sermon:**
    - **Definition:** Specific aspects of the sermon that were particularly strong or effective.
    - **Considerations:** Identify and describe the key strengths and positive elements of the sermon.

    Comments: _____

    _____

16. **Areas for Improvement:**
    - **Definition:** Specific areas where the sermon could be improved or refined.
    - **Considerations:** Identify and describe aspects of the sermon that could be enhanced or done differently for greater impact.

    Comments: _____

    _____

Final Thoughts:

Based on the sermon, do you believe this candidate would be an effective lead pastor for our congregation? Why or why not?

_____

Signature: _____ **Date:** _____

This evaluation tool helps the search committee objectively assess the effectiveness and impact of each candidate's sermon, ensuring a comprehensive review of their preaching abilities.

Considerations for Compensation of a Lead Pastor for a Large Church

Introduction

Compensation for a lead pastor is a critical aspect of ensuring that the church attracts and retains a qualified and dedicated leader. This document outlines the key considerations to be considered when determining the compensation package for a lead pastor of a large church. These considerations ensure that the compensation is fair, competitive, and reflective of the responsibilities and expectations associated with the role. This should be approved by the official board, or the entity in the church that decides compensation.

---

1. Base Salary

Factors to Consider:

- Experience and Qualifications: The pastor's level of education, years of pastoral experience, and relevant certifications or training.
- Size and Budget of the Church: Larger congregations and higher church budgets generally warrant higher salaries.
- Geographic Location: Cost of living in the church's area.
- Comparable Positions: Salaries of lead pastors in similar-sized churches within the denomination and region. www.churchsalary.com and https://info.vanderbloemen.com/download-2023-salary-guide provide up to date salary guides.

Recommended Actions:

- Conduct a salary survey of similar churches.
- Consider the pastor's previous salary and any increase needed to match the new role's demands.

---

2. Housing Allowance

Factors to Consider:

- Cost of Housing: Local real estate and rental market conditions.
- Parsonage: Whether the church provides a parsonage and associated costs (maintenance, utilities, etc.).
- IRS Guidelines: Ensure compliance with tax regulations regarding housing allowances for clergy.
- Recommended Actions:
- Review the current housing market to determine an appropriate allowance.
- Provide options if a parsonage is not available, such as a housing stipend.

3. Benefits

Health and Dental Insurance:

- Comprehensive coverage for the pastor and their family.
- Consideration of premium costs, deductibles, and out-of-pocket expenses.

Retirement Plan:

- Contributions to a retirement plan, such as a 403(b) or similar.
- Matching contributions or church-funded retirement plans.

Life and Disability Insurance:

- Adequate life insurance coverage.
- Short-term and long-term disability insurance.

Recommended Actions:

- Review benefits packages offered by similar-sized churches.
- Consult with insurance providers to customize a benefits package.

4. Professional Development

Factors to Consider:

- Continuing Education: Support for theological training, leadership development, and other relevant courses.
- Conferences and Retreats: Attendance at denominational or other relevant conferences.
- Sabbaticals: Periodic sabbaticals for rest and renewal.

Recommended Actions:

- Allocate a budget for professional development.
- Establish clear guidelines and expectations for professional development activities.

5. Paid Time Off (PTO)

Factors to Consider:

- Vacation Time: Adequate vacation time to ensure rest and family time.
- Sick Leave: Provisions for illness and medical appointments.
- Personal Days: Additional days for personal matters or family emergencies.

Recommended Actions:

- Benchmark against PTO policies of similar churches.
- Ensure policies are clearly communicated and consistently applied.

6. Ministry-Related Expenses

Factors to Consider:

- Automobile Allowance: Reimbursement for mileage or a car allowance for ministry-related travel.

- Professional Expenses: Budget for books, resources, and other ministry-related materials.
- Entertainment and Hospitality: Funds for hosting church events or meeting with congregation members.

Recommended Actions:

- Establish a reimbursement policy for ministry-related expenses.
- Review IRS guidelines for reimbursable expenses.

7. Performance and Merit Increases

Factors to Consider:

- Annual Reviews: Regular performance evaluations to assess effectiveness and accomplishments.
- Merit Increases: Salary adjustments based on performance and contributions to the church's growth and mission.

Recommended Actions:

- Develop a transparent performance review process.
- Link merit increases to specific performance metrics and achievements.

Conclusion

Compensation for a lead pastor should be thoughtfully and carefully considered to ensure it meets the needs of the pastor while aligning with the church's financial capabilities and goals. By taking into account these key considerations, the church can create a comprehensive and competitive compensation package that honors the pastor's commitment and service.

Approval and Review:

The church's finance committee and governing board should review and approve this document.

Regular reviews should be conducted to ensure the compensation package remains competitive and fair.

Offboarding Document for Lead Pastor

Introduction

This document provides a structured process to ensure a smooth and respectful transition as the Lead Pastor leaves the church. It outlines the necessary steps to facilitate an orderly departure and maintain continuity within the church community.

Acknowledgment:

We are grateful for the service and leadership that [Pastor's Name] has provided to [Church Name]. This offboarding process aims to honor their contributions and ensure a seamless transition.

Notice and Communication Plan

Notice Period:

- Standard notice period as per the employment agreement.
- Official resignation letter submission date.

Communication Plan:

- Announce the departure to church staff and leadership team.
- Inform the congregation through a formal announcement (during service, email, newsletter).
- Address any concerns or questions from the congregation and staff.

Transition Plan

Interim Leadership:

- Appoint an interim pastor or designate a leadership team member to assume responsibilities temporarily.
- Define the interim leadership's role and responsibilities.

Ongoing Projects:

- List current projects and initiatives led by the outgoing pastor.
- Assign temporary leaders for these projects until a permanent replacement is found.

Key Dates:

- Last working day of the outgoing pastor.
- Key milestones in the transition period.

Handover of Responsibilities

Handover Document:

- Prepare a detailed handover document outlining ongoing tasks, projects, and responsibilities.

Meetings and Introductions:

- Conduct meetings with key staff, ministry leaders, and stakeholders to facilitate knowledge transfer.
- Introduce interim leadership to key contacts and stakeholders.

Documentation:

- Ensure all relevant documents, passwords, and access information are transferred to the interim leadership or appropriate staff members.

Exit Interview

Purpose:

- Gain feedback on the pastor's experience and insights on the church's operations.
- Identify areas for improvement and opportunities for growth.

Interview Questions:

- What were the highlights and challenges of your tenure?
- Do you have any recommendations for the church moving forward?
- How can we improve the support and resources provided to the pastoral team?

Final Payroll and Benefits

Payroll:

- Calculate and process the final paycheck, including any accrued vacation or leave time.
- Ensure all financial obligations are met in accordance with the employment agreement.

Benefits:

- Review the status of health insurance, retirement plans, and other benefits.
- Provide information on the continuation of benefits, such as COBRA, if applicable.

Return of Church Property

Items to be Returned:

- Create a checklist of items to be returned including:
- Church keys and access cards
- Office equipment (computer, phone, etc.)
- Church-owned vehicles
- Any other church property
- Schedule a time for the return and inspection of items.

Farewell Arrangements

Farewell Event:

- Plan a farewell event to honor and celebrate the outgoing pastor's service.
- Involve the congregation in expressing gratitude and well wishes.

Gifts and Acknowledgments:

- Consider presenting a farewell gift or token of appreciation.
- Provide a platform for personal messages and acknowledgments from the congregation and staff.

Post-Departure Considerations

Contact Information:

- Obtain updated contact information for future correspondence.
- Provide a point of contact for any post-departure questions or follow-ups.

Ongoing Support:

- Offer pastoral care and support for the outgoing pastor and their family during the transition.
- Maintain a positive and supportive relationship with the outgoing pastor.

Succession Planning:

- Begin the search for a new lead pastor following the established pastoral search process.
- Keep the congregation informed about the progress of the search and interim leadership arrangements.

Notes:

Ensure all steps are conducted with respect and sensitivity.

Maintain open communication throughout the transition period to address any concerns or issues promptly.

Thank you, [Pastor's Name], for your dedicated service and leadership. You will always be a valued member of our [Church Name] family.

Bibliography

Bullock, W. (2013). *Your next pastor: guidelines for finding God's person for your church.* GPH.

Cochran, Nicole. (2024). 7 Elements To Include On Your Pastor Search Website. https://www.vanderbloemen.com/blog/7-elements-to-include-on-your-pastor-search-website

Dingman, Robert W. (1994). In Search of a Leader: The Complete Search Committee Guidebook. West Village, CA: Lakeside Books.

Indiana District Assemblies of God. (2022). *Transition Manual: A Guide for Congregations in Pastoral Transition.*

Vanderbloemen Search Group. (2020). *Comprehensive Back Ground Checks.* https://www.vanderbloemen.com/background-check?hsCtaTracking=02da72ce-388a-4391-b917-f03f46b342ff%7C15df1dbb-3577-46b3-9d89-06d0a7261674

Vanderbloemen Search Group. (2024). 6 Mistakes Search Committees Make When Looking For A Senior Pastor. https://www.vanderbloemen.com/blog/6-mistakes-search-committees-make-when-looking-for-a-senior-pastor

Vanderbloemen Search Group. (2023). https://www.vanderbloemen.com/blog/right-hiring-route

About John Utley

Dr. John W. Utley holds a Doctorate in Strategic Christian Ministry from Liberty University. His extensive leadership includes founding two churches, serving in key pastoral roles at four additional churches, and acting as a transition specialist for numerous churches and non-profit organizations. Renowned for guiding institutions through challenging transitions, Dr. Utley is also a sought-after mentor for pastors and a strategic consultant for churches. He resides in Fort Worth, Texas, with his wife, Susan, to whom he has been married for over thirty-eight years. Together, they have three married children and three grandchildren. He has written three books, *When God Says Nothing, Amazing God,* and his first fiction novel, *Meeting Jack Cash.*

If your church or non-profit organization is in need of a seasoned transition consultant, don't hesitate to reach out to Dr. Utley for expert guidance and support.

Dr. John Utley may be reached at john.utley@cottonhouse.press or by calling 574-370-3661.